CRANSTON
—— AND ITS ——
MAYORS

A HISTORY

CRANSTON
AND ITS
MAYORS

A HISTORY

STEVEN FRIAS

Published by The History Press
Charleston, SC 29403
www.historypress.net

Copyright © 2011 by Steven Frias
All rights reserved

First published 2011

Manufactured in the United States

ISBN 978.1.60949.322.6

Library of Congress Cataloging-in-Publication Data

Frias, Steven.
Cranston and its mayors : a history / Steven Frias.
p. cm.
Includes bibliographical references and index.
ISBN 978-1-60949-322-6
1. Mayors--Rhode Island--Cranston--Biography. 2. Cranston (R.I.)--Biography. 3. Cranston (R.I.)--Politics and government. 4. Cranston (R.I.)--History. 5. Cranston (R.I.)--Economic conditions. 6. Social change--Rhode Island--Cranston--History. 7. City and town life--Rhode Island--Cranston--History. I. Title.
F89.C8F75 2011
974.5'1--dc23
2011031487

Notice: The information in this book is true and complete to the best of our knowledge. It is offered without guarantee on the part of the author or The History Press. The author and The History Press disclaim all liability in connection with the use of this book.

All rights reserved. No part of this book may be reproduced or transmitted in any form whatsoever without prior written permission from the publisher except in the case of brief quotations embodied in critical articles and reviews.

Contents

Preface   7

Beginnings: 1638–1910

Establishing a Town   9
The Cost of Freedom   11
Industrialization and Division   14
Becoming a City   18

Growth: 1910–1934

Edward M. Sullivan   23
John W. Horton   27
Arthur A. Rhodes   31
Frank C. Speck   36
Frederick A. Jones   38

Transformation: 1935–1960

Ernest L. Sprague   43
William G. Lind   50
Hoyt W. Lark   53
George R. Beane   58
John Turnbull   61
Earl A. Colvin   63

Contents

CHALLENGES: 1961–1984

Francis R. Dailey	69
James DiPrete Jr.	73
James L. Taft Jr.	83
Edward D. DiPrete	90

CRISIS: 1985–PRESENT

Michael A. Traficante	97
John O'Leary	113
Stephen P. Laffey	120
Michael T. Napolitano	129
Allan W. Fung	133
Notes	139
Index	157
About the Author	159

Preface

From the War of Independence to the Civil War and from colonization to the Industrial Revolution, Cranston played a memorable role. These aspects of Cranston's history from the eighteenth and nineteenth centuries are preserved. However, there seems to be a gap in the narration of Cranston history when it comes to the twentieth century. This gap is also apparent when it comes to Rhode Island history. This work is an attempt to recount Cranston's history with a focus on more modern times. Because Cranston was Rhode Island's first suburb—or as one proud local newspaper editorialist called it, "a city of homes"—this history will hopefully illuminate important aspects of the state's modern history as well.[1]

This history will not be a narrative touching on wars for freedom or the excitement of technological innovation. However, like Tacitus, the ancient Roman historian, I anticipate that my history of the small, almost mundane, events that occurred in this small city in this small state will help demonstrate that small, unnoticed events can result in vast changes with profound effects on a community. Although this is a history of a small city, what occurs in local communities has a large impact. As noted in one forgotten editorial in a long-defunct local newspaper, if local communities "are run in a loose and careless way, the same spirit will spread to the state and the nation."[2]

What this history may lack in inspiration or heroism, I hope to make up in relevance to current events. Local history tends to be celebratory, in order to bring forth a sense of pride, or more pictorial, so as to arouse feelings of nostalgia. I do not pretend that this history is comprehensive in the sense that it addresses all that occurred in Cranston. It is not a

Preface

history of what occurred in a community as much as it is a history of how a community was governed. The mayors who occupied Cranston City Hall are at the center of this story, just as city hall lies at the center of Cranston. Government reflects its community, but as this narrative will show, government also subtly reshapes its community. Through these pages, the reader will see how a government incrementally expands. The reasons will vary and the speed will fluctuate, but the direction will remain constant. As a result, there is much more in this history about Cranston's finances than about its historic buildings.

Like Thucydides, the ancient Greek historian, my aspiration for this book is that it will be useful to those who desire knowledge of the past as an aid to the interpretation of the future, because human nature being what it is, the past will repeat itself. Although Cranston City Hall may have a new roof, the reader will find that what goes on beneath that roof today resembles what transpired there in the past. As a result, I have had to record some unpleasant events without trying to present them in the best possible light. In other words, this history paints a picture of Cranston's more modern history, with "warts and all." Accordingly, I have reserved for this narrative an account of what I believe were the most important and most relevant events in terms of how Cranston was administered, particularly over the past century, in the hope that it will prove instructive to us in the present and to those who will live in the century to come.

Beginnings

1638–1910

Establishing a Town

1638–1754

When it comes to public affairs, history is little more than a chronicle of quarrels. At times, these quarrels turn violent or have momentous consequences. As for the disputes surrounding the establishment of the town of Cranston, they were merely prolonged squabbles.

In 1638, just two years after Roger Williams founded Providence, the first settlers made their homes near the Pawtuxet River in present-day Cranston. From the outset, this small village gained a reputation for "political troublemaking."[1] In 1643, differences with settlers in Providence caused Pawtuxet residents to place themselves under the jurisdiction of the neighboring Massachusetts colony. This association with Massachusetts lasted until 1658. After switching allegiances back to Providence, Pawtuxet became the center of a long dispute over property rights and boundaries. In order to establish his colony, Roger Williams had made two land purchases from the Indians that were governed by deeds. One was called the "Grand Purchase of Providence," while the second was called the "Pawtuxet Purchase." The precise boundaries of the Pawtuxet Purchase would be a source of controversy and litigation that extended beyond the lives of the early settlers. It was not until 1696 that the Pawtuxet River officially became the southern boundary of the Pawtuxet Purchase, while it took until 1712 for the western boundary of the Pawtuxet Purchase to be established. These boundaries would eventually become the southern and western borders of Cranston.

Even before its boundaries were known, there was a movement among these early settlers to establish their own town. Beginning in 1660, petitions were being circulated to have the area now known as Cranston separated from Providence. The motivation behind these petitions did not arise from civic pride or lofty principles but rather from the desire for convenience. In the time of horses and poor roads, a trek of about ten miles into Providence in order to attend a town meeting, record a land sale or file a will could be a nuisance. Thus, the impetus behind the creation of the town of Cranston was the wish of its residents to engage in governmental affairs with less inconvenience.

The petitions of these early settlers were not granted because they could not agree on a name for their new town. These settlers divided themselves into four parochial bands espousing four different Indian names: Pawtuxet, Mashapaug, Mashantatuck and Pocasset. For nearly a century, the bickering over a name for their new town continued, and as a result, the residents remained part of the town of Providence. Finally, in 1754, a compromise was reached. An Indian name for the new town was discarded, and instead, the name of Lynn was chosen, since many of the early settlers in present-day Cranston had come from Lynn, Massachusetts. Although they had finally reached an agreement on a name for their new town, they still needed the approval of the Rhode Island General Assembly. On June 14, 1754, the General Assembly approved the creation of a new town to the south of Providence, but with a name none had suggested in the past. On the petition creating the new town, a line was drawn through the name of Lynn, and in its place was substituted the name of Cranston.[2]

Since the reasons for this last-minute substitution are unclear, they have led to a debate among historians over for whom the town of Cranston was named. Some historians have stated that the town of Cranston was named after Governor Samuel Cranston, the longest-serving governor in Rhode Island history. Governor Cranston served for nearly three decades, from 1698 to 1727, before he died in office. During his time as governor, Cranston had maintained Rhode Island's existence as a separate colony while increasing the powers of the General Assembly over the colony's economic affairs. Although Governor Cranston's service merits recognition, he had little connection to the area now called Cranston, and by the time Cranston was incorporated as a town, he had been dead for nearly three decades. Instead, some historians argue that the town of Cranston was actually named after another man named Thomas Cranston. This member of the Cranston family was the grandson of Governor Samuel Cranston, but more importantly, he was the Speaker of the House of Representatives at the time the General Assembly approved the petition creating a new town to the south of Providence. As evidence, they point to the first page of Cranston's first Town Record Book, which contains the inscription, "The gift of Thomas Cranston to the town called Cranston."[3] Furthermore, they note that the idea of naming a town after a living politician was not out of the ordinary since it was done for other Rhode Island towns established in the second half of the eighteenth century.

As a result, a century-long dispute over what to name a proposed town situated to the south of Providence has turned into a long-running historical debate about which member of the Cranston political dynasty garnered the honor of having the town of Cranston named after him. It is a debate that will never be conclusively resolved. However, for those with a more cynical or perhaps a more realistic view of human nature, it seems more likely that the town of Cranston was named after a living politician who possessed the influence to ensure passage of a long-sought-after petition rather than being an honor granted to a long-deceased government official who did not possess any powers to affect pending legislation from his grave.

The debate will continue over whom the General Assembly intended to honor when it bestowed the name of Cranston on the new town. But there can be no debating the fact that it was not the residents of this new town who chose the name of Cranston but rather state legislators in the give and take of politics. It was in this manner that the town of Cranston came into existence.

The Cost of Freedom

1754–1790

When Cranston became a town, its citizens elected a town council. However, the citizenry of Cranston, made up of mostly farmers, left the most significant issues, such as taxation, to be decided through town meetings. These town meetings held at the taverns of Caleb Arnold and Nehemiah Knight were at times boisterous, due in part to the consumption of rum at these events, but they reflected pure democracy in action. In 1774, in response to the Boston Tea Party, the British Parliament enacted the Coercive Acts, which, among other things, changed the form of government in the Massachusetts

The first town meetings were held at the tavern of Caleb Arnold. *Courtesy of Cranston Historical Society.*

colony and severely restricted town meetings in that colony as well. Colonists throughout America viewed the Coercive Acts as a threat to their freedoms, and in Cranston, they expressed their outrage by adopting a resolution in opposition to the measures passed by the British Parliament. In the following year, as differences escalated, Cranston pledged its support to the newly formed Continental Congress and expressed its opposition to British attempts at "taxing Americans without their consent."[4] Fighting soon broke out between American colonists and British troops, and a year later, in 1776, the American colonies declared their independence from Great Britain.

In support of the fight for independence, Cranston supplied iron and enlisted soldiers. However, raw materials and brave recruits are not enough to win a war. Money is necessary to pay soldiers and to supply them. Cranston, like other communities, obtained the necessary revenues to pay for the war effort through higher taxation and heavy borrowing. To help win a war for political independence, Cranston became economically dependent on debt. After the Battle of Yorktown in 1781, which was won by the Americans with help from French troops that had reached the battle by marching through Cranston, the American colonies became independent, but Cranston and Rhode Island were nearly bankrupt as a result of the war.

When a government is heavily in debt, it can repay the debt by enacting higher taxes and adopting fiscal austerity measures, or it can simply default on the debt. Sometimes a government will claim it is repaying the debt when, in fact, it is repudiating it. This occurs when the government prints money in order to pay back debt, thereby triggering inflation. Inflation would be the path chosen by Rhode Island with the support of Cranston's citizens.

In 1786, the Country Party, led by Jonathan Hazard, captured power in Rhode Island after campaigning on the compassionate-sounding slogan of "To Relieve the Distressed" and pledging to print paper money in order to pay off the war debt. With the full support of Cranston, the Rhode Island General Assembly began issuing paper money. This inflationary policy proved politically popular because it not only eliminated the war debt but also reduced the burden on the heavily indebted farmers, who were the majority in Rhode Island. In effect, inflation becomes the means not only to pay for a costly war but also to alleviate the plight of the downtrodden. However, merchants, who were the creditors, fled Rhode Island rather than accept paper money that rapidly fell in value. The General Assembly passed laws making it a crime not to accept this declining currency, but even the threat of punishment could not prevent economic reality from causing the value of this paper money to fall further. Eventually, Rhode Island's paper currency fell to a market value of less than eight cents on the dollar. This hyperinflation caused Rhode Island to devolve into a barter economy, and shortages of grain occurred. While this paper money scheme proved politically popular with a majority of Rhode Island voters, it was denounced as odious and deplorable throughout the rest of the nation. In fact, the example of Rhode Island served as a favorite weapon of advocates for a new federal Constitution, one in which states were prohibited from issuing paper money. Rhode Island took no part in drafting a new federal Constitution and, once it was proposed, stubbornly refused to ratify it, with the citizens of Cranston voting unanimously against adopting it. In 1790, after the war debt had been paid off with paper money and with the newly established federal government threatening Rhode Island with trade sanctions, Rhode Island finally but barely ratified the new federal Constitution, with the delegates from Cranston in opposition to the end.[5]

Cranston supported the war for independence to prevent taxation without representation. But in order to pay the debt arising from that war, Cranston tried to avoid higher taxation by resorting to the expediency of inflation. This would not be the last time that Cranston and its leaders would support policies that were politically expedient but proved to be economically damaging.

Industrialization and Division

1790–1892

After persevering through revolutionary warfare and chaotic inflation, Cranston turned its attention to the matters that preoccupied a small agricultural community. During the late eighteenth and early nineteenth centuries, heated debates at town meetings occurred over tending to the poor, maintaining roads and providing for education. During this time, the poor were auctioned off to those residents who could feed and clothe them at the lowest expense to the town. In 1839, the town's poor were sent to live on a farm bought by the town, where they worked and lived under stringent rules. It would not be until well into the twentieth century that a more liberal and open-handed approach by the federal and state government caused life in poverty to become more agreeable.[6]

Caring for the poor was not the only topic of debate. Poor road conditions were also a matter of concern. Attempts to raise taxes to pay for road improvements were voted down at town meetings, but eventually, in 1798, Cranston allocated $1,000 for highway repairs. Cranston citizens then continued to support expenditures on roads, and in 1819, Park Avenue was built, thereby connecting the eastern and western ends of the town. Arguments over expending money on public highways were soon followed by disagreements over expenditures for public schools. Originally, schooling was solely a private matter, but in 1828, the Rhode Island General Assembly enacted a law to open public schools funded from state license fees and lottery proceeds. At their town meeting, Cranston's residents initially opposed raising taxes to fund public schools, but in 1833, $500 from property taxes was budgeted for public schools, an amount that would grow year after year. These town meetings of a small, rustic community would soon be overshadowed by the clouds of industrialization.

Rhode Island was an ideal place for the American Industrial Revolution to commence. Energy was available from Rhode Island's rivers to power machines. Labor was inexpensive because farming was so unprofitable due to Rhode Island's poor agricultural soils. When the available pool of labor from the countryside was exhausted, immigrants from abroad gladly crossed the ocean to work in Rhode Island rather than remaining in their homelands to suffer from starvation.[7] Government regulation of business was almost nonexistent in Rhode Island, with manufacturers given "almost complete freedom of action." Taxation was so minimal

Beginnings

that "Rhode Islanders went for long periods without having to pay state property taxes at all."[8]

One of the first Rhode Islanders to take advantage of this favorable business climate was a Cranston farmer called William Sprague II. In 1808, he converted his small gristmill near the Pocasset River into a cotton mill. Eventually, he became owner of an array of enterprises, and in 1824, he established the Print Works in Cranston. The Print Works was Cranston's first important industrial enterprise and played a central role in the lives of those Cranston residents who lived in its mill village. William Sprague II and his descendants went on to create a vast business empire that extended beyond textiles into fields such as banks, railroads and horse-drawn streetcars. Economic wealth leads to political influence; the accumulation of one leads to an increase in the other. For three generations, the Spragues weaved together the threads of their economic interests with the strands of their political ambitions into one fabric that enveloped Cranston for decades, until it all unraveled in the Panic of 1873.

The Spragues began dabbling in politics after the Rhode Island General Assembly passed legislation in 1831 increasing taxation on banks owned by William Sprague II. In 1842, after holding various other political offices, including governor, William Sprague III, the son of William Sprague II, became a U.S. senator. This occurred, in part, because of Sprague's apparent support for expanding voting rights to those who did not own

The Print Works was Cranston's first important industrial enterprise. In 1996, the Print Works decided to close its manufacturing plant due to high costs. *Courtesy of Cranston Historical Society.*

property. However, Sprague's support for expanding voting rights was not altogether based on noble motives. Because of the lack of a true secret ballot, Sprague, through his agents, could influence, if not control, the votes of his employees.[9] Sprague's workers supported his political endeavors either out of gratitude to their benefactor or from fear of an employer who had power over their lives like a feudal overlord. When advocates for expanded suffrage, led by Thomas Dorr, established their own government under a "People's Constitution," Sprague turned against their cause and used his influence to prevent his employees from supporting Dorr.[10] Dorr's rebellion failed.

Shortly thereafter, in 1844, William Sprague III's political career ended abruptly when he resigned from the U.S. Senate in order to manage the Sprague family's business interests after his brother, Amasa Sprague, was brutally murdered. It was alleged that the motive for the murder of Amasa Sprague stemmed from the use of his considerable influence over the Cranston Town Council to deny the renewal of a liquor license to a nearby shop owned by an Irish immigrant on the grounds that some of Sprague's employees were reporting to work intoxicated. Years later, in 1860, the Spragues would reenter political office when William Sprague IV, the son of the murdered Amasa Sprague, used his ample wealth to be elected governor at the age of twenty-nine. The next year, Governor Sprague personally led Rhode Island troops into the first battle of the American Civil War at Bull Run, where the Union army was soundly defeated and fled from the battlefield in a panic, but Sprague, whose horse was shot from under him, was acclaimed a hero and went on to be elected a U.S. senator.

In the 1860s, the American Civil War nearly caused the nation to split into Northern and Southern halves. At about this same time, urbanization arising from industrialization divided eastern Cranston from western Cranston and would ultimately lead to the separation of a portion of eastern Cranston from the remainder of the town. When Cranston was a town, it originally included the neighborhoods of South Providence and Elmwood. In 1854, the residents of Elmwood favored annexation with the city of Providence. Their efforts were defeated, but to placate these residents, it was agreed to move the town clerk's office to Elmwood Avenue, and two voting districts for town meetings were established at different ends of the town. However, these accommodations proved insufficient because the interests of Elmwood and South Providence residents were diverging from the rest of Cranston.

At this time, South Providence was very industrialized. In particular, a South Providence neighborhood called Dogtown was the site of "foul piggeries" and slaughterhouses. The Cranston Town Council attempted to regulate and prohibit these sorts of nuisances, but the orders of town officials were ignored. In addition, newspapers reported "muggings and burglars" and disorderly conduct at liquor establishments in South Providence. The Cranston Town Council's attempts to address these problems were inadequate since Cranston only paid for ten police constables and eighteen special police constables. By comparison, the city of Providence had a police force of about one hundred. In addition, the city of Providence had a large fire department, sewers and street lighting, while Cranston did not have this level of municipal services. Most of Cranston's population did not see the need for these services, nor did they have the desire to pay higher taxes for them. Consequently, the residents of South Providence and Elmwood were "like city dwellers without city services." Accordingly, in 1868, the voters of both the eastern and western sections of Cranston agreed to the annexation of South Providence and Elmwood by the city of Providence. The final changes to the boundary between Cranston and Providence occurred later, when Cranston ceded small portions of its territory to Providence in 1873, 1887 and 1892 in order to create and expand Roger Williams Park.[11]

The separation of South Providence and Elmwood from Cranston had a dramatic impact on Cranston. Cranston's population was reduced from 9,177 to 4,822. The town's limited municipal services were slashed when its police constable force was reduced by nearly two-thirds. Cranston's property tax rate was cut from ninety cents per $100 to seventy-five cents per $100. Lastly, Cranston's town hall was moved to the rear of a store owned by the Spragues, a suggestive symbol of the sway the Spragues had over Cranston.[12]

Cranston Town Hall would remain on Sprague property until 1886, when a new town hall was built in Knightsville on the site of a tavern where town meetings had been held at the beginning of the nineteenth century. By the end of the nineteenth century, the Spragues' far-flung commercial empire had collapsed in the Panic of 1873 and with it their influence over Cranston. The Panic of 1873 was caused by a contraction in the money supply, which raised the cost of borrowing, thereby harming any business—like railroads—that carried heavy debt loads. The Spragues, who were heavily dependent on credit for financing their diverse business interests, could not make their debt payments and went bankrupt. Zechariah Chafee was made the trustee over the Spragues' enterprises, and his controversial actions led to years of litigation. Chafee proved to be an "incompetent" trustee who "betrayed his trust and enriched himself by defrauding both the Sprague family and the creditors who appointed them." It was only through "legal maneuvers and special favors" that Chafee "managed to save himself from indictment."[13] For the Sprague dynasty, which had produced two men who were elected to both the offices of governor and U.S. senator, its glory days had come to a close. Chafee, the man who oversaw the end of it, in turn sired a wealthy political dynasty of his own that produced two men who would both eventually be elected to the offices of governor and U.S. senator, just like the Spragues.

The influence of the Spragues over Cranston may have ended, but the debate over the appropriate level of government services has never ceased. At the beginning of the nineteenth century, Cranston town meetings were consumed by heated debates over the proper level of government spending for the poor, roads and public education. The desire for more government services increased as urbanization arose after the advent of industrialization. By the middle of the nineteenth century, the boundaries of Cranston were being redrawn over a fundamental disagreement about the proper level of government services. During the twentieth century, Cranston would irrevocably be changed by government services.

BECOMING A CITY

1892–1910

Like much of Cranston's history, the manner in which Cranston became a city was not ordinary or without controversy. Although Cranston became a town in 1754, its population did not grow rapidly until the second half of the nineteenth century. During the Civil War, the Spragues established a line of horse-drawn streetcars from Providence to Cranston. In 1892, this streetcar system, which had been powered by slow horses, was electrified. The "revolutionary force" of electricity created "new mobility" and led to real estate speculation wherever the electric trolley cars passed as businessmen and professionals who worked in Providence sought suburban settings in which to live.[14] In 1880, Cranston was a town of 5,940 residents, but by 1895, it had nearly doubled to 10,575, and by 1910, it had doubled yet again, standing at 21,283. Cranston was a growing suburb of Providence at a time of "unparalleled prosperity" for that city, when it was "one of the major cities of the world," and Rhode Island was ranked "second in per capita wealth of all the United States."[15]

As Cranston's population grew, so did demands for more municipal services. During the 1890s, Cranston began a "road building era" that led

Beginnings

to the widening and rebuilding of many roads.[16] There was an increase in funding of the public school system, and Cranston for the first time opened its own high school. As Cranston rapidly changed, some of its citizens decided that the form of municipal government should also change from a town to a city. This change in government would be driven, in part, by the desire to increase municipal services.

The issue of altering Cranston's form of government from that of a town to a city was not merely a matter of semantics or prestige but of substance and principles. In a town form of government, citizens could directly control the financial management of the community through the town meeting. Furthermore, at the time, there existed a provision in the Rhode Island Constitution known as the Bourn Amendment, which established a property requirement in order to vote in city council elections. As a result, a change from a town to a city form of government at the turn of the twentieth century in Rhode Island was a step toward less public participation in government.

During this time period, the Republican Party dominated the Cranston Town Council, and in turn, the party was dominated by prominent citizens such as John M. Dean, a wealthy merchant, and Frank L. Budlong, a large landowner. Dean, Budlong and many other leaders of the Cranston Republican Party were involved in real estate development. These developers

Cranston's town hall from 1886 to 1910 and its city hall from 1910 to 1937. *Courtesy of Cranston Historical Society.*

believed that an increase in municipal services was "crucial to their attempt to attract home buyers" to Cranston. As Cranston's municipal spending and taxes grew, the control of these developers was challenged. At town meetings filled with "wrangling" and "yelling," opponents of higher taxes were able to muster large showings to frustrate the ability of the Republicans to govern the town.[17] Finding that the town meetings had become unmanageable, the Republicans pursued the granting of a city charter to Cranston. In 1895, the issue of whether Cranston should become a city was put to the voters in a referendum that was defeated by a narrow margin.

Fear had created an unlikely alliance. The millworkers centered in Knightsville, who feared being disenfranchised under a city form of government, joined with the frugal farmers of western Cranston, who feared a city form of government would lead to more government spending and higher taxes, to defeat the referendum. A second attempt was made in 1904, and once again, the voters of Cranston rejected making Cranston a city, this time by a wide margin. After a series of town meetings in 1908 and 1909 had led to spending limitations being imposed, Cranston schools were closed for a few weeks. Spurred by this dramatic loss of an important governmental service, as well as by the twin desires to maintain power and gain profit, leading Republicans and real estate developers had a "secret meeting" in Providence where they decided to resort to other means to obtain a city charter.[18] Although repeatedly defeated in their efforts, the leading Republicans of Cranston remained undeterred. Their cause had been unpopular, but their persistence proved more potent. On March 10, 1910, they eventually succeeded in persuading the General Assembly to impose on Cranston a city form of government without a vote of its residents. Thus, Cranston became a city, not through the consent of its residents, but through an unpopular state mandate contrived by its public officials, a most troubling start to Cranston's history as a city.

Elections are predictably contentious, but their outcomes are not always predictable. Under the new city charter, the first mayoral election was scheduled for April 19, 1910. For mayor, the Republicans nominated Dean. As for the Democrats, their mayoral nominee was Edward M. Sullivan, a thirty-five-year-old son of Irish immigrants born in the Cranston Print Works village who was a journalist-turned-attorney. As a journalist, Sullivan had been an outspoken critic of how Cranston was managed by the town council, and as an attorney, he had battled with Republican leaders at town meetings, where he "crusaded against high taxes and excessive spending."[19]

Dean was the clear favorite in this race. Cranston had voted soundly Republican for many years at all levels of government. In Sullivan's favor was his message. Sullivan accused the Republican town council of having financially mismanaged Cranston for nearly two decades, leading to deficits, accumulated debt and overspending by Cranston Public Schools, a recurring issue in Cranston politics, especially in recent decades. Also, Sullivan opposed raising property taxes, a position that is always popular, even if it is not always credible. But the decisive issue in this campaign was the adoption of the city charter without voter approval. Sullivan had opposed the move by Cranston's Republicans to have the state impose a city charter on Cranston, and voter anger over this issue had not cooled.

Although Sullivan had waged an aggressive campaign, most observers expected another Republican electoral triumph in Cranston. Instead, Sullivan defeated Dean by the narrow margin of 30 votes, 1,195 to 1,165, or 50.6 percent to 49.4 percent. The victory of Sullivan in Cranston was stunning. At the time of the election, Cranston's entire delegation to the General Assembly was Republican, as were all Rhode Island's statewide officers and Rhode Island's entire federal delegation. Even the mayors of Providence, Pawtucket and Central Falls were Republicans in 1910.

For some, Sullivan's victory was inspiring, since it demonstrated that even in the most difficult of circumstances the remarkable is possible when courage and relentless energy are joined with talent to further a cause popular with an enraged public. For others, the defeat of Cranston's Republicans, in the city's first election under the charter they had long sought, confirmed the warning made in an ancient fable: "Be careful what you wish for." But to all, Cranston's first mayoral election showed that, at least on occasion, those in authority are held accountable when they ignore the wishes of the people.

GROWTH

1910–1934

EDWARD M. SULLIVAN

1910–1914

Unsurprisingly, after a contentious mayoral election, Cranston's first transfer of power was a rancorous episode. Under the new Cranston City Charter, various officials who were appointed by the town council would remain in office until January 1911, regardless of the outcome of the April 1910 city election. According to Sullivan, some of these hold-over appointees of the Republican-controlled town council engaged in various obstructionist activities, such as when the town council–appointed police chief began enforcing long disregarded blue laws for store hours while claiming the Sullivan administration was behind this new crackdown. Sullivan blasted these hold-over appointees by attacking the city auditor as "notoriously incompetent" and accusing the police chief of working "in full uniform at the polls on election day" for the Republicans.[1]

Unable to remove the chief of police and other officers appointed by the town council, Sullivan had the Democrat-controlled city council strip these officers of their duties, deny them compensation and transfer their powers to others, while leaving these hold-over officials with empty titles, thus turning them into trifles.

This would not be the last change Sullivan would make in the office of police chief. Sullivan would quickly clash with his own newly appointed police chief. He would replace him in 1912 with a new police chief, who was confirmed by the city council, with Sullivan breaking a tie vote.[2] Controversy would continue to surround the police department throughout Sullivan's mayoral tenure.

Although fighting over governmental positions generated much controversy, Sullivan's primary concern was the financial condition of the city. Sullivan saw "the great problem in the government of Cranston" as "the management of its finances." He noted that "the financial history of Cranston has been a record of continuous annual deficits, which have operated to swell the permanent debt of the municipality." He placed the blame on two decades of "incompetence and mismanagement" by the Republican-controlled town council. Alarmed by deficit spending and mounting debt, an alarm that is still heard today, Sullivan had the Democrat-controlled city council adopt a financial policy "to limit the expenditures for current running expenses to the current income," a rule that has proven hard for many elected officials to follow. Fearing higher taxes, Sullivan pledged to obey the "mandate from the taxpayers to limit our expenditures" so as not raise the property tax rate above the then existing level of $1.30 per $100. He believed that higher taxes would harm the growth of the city, while a stable tax rate would provide incentive for businesses to come to Cranston, thereby causing the tax base to grow.

As for spending on government services, Sullivan thought that "the increased demands" for "more police protection, street lighting [and] highways" would be paid from the "natural increase" in the property tax base, which would "provide sufficient additional revenue" without "increasing the property tax rate." With the help of a rapidly expanding tax base, in his nearly four years in office, Sullivan never raised the property tax rate while achieving balanced budgets and lowering the debt level of the city. With justifiable pride, Sullivan could state that "the greatest achievement" of his administration was "the placing of the finances of the city upon a firm and sound basis."[3]

Although Sullivan admittedly had not given Cranston "days of tranquility and peace," in November 1910, the voters showed their approval by reelecting him with 56.4 percent of the vote while carrying all four wards. After defeating his foes at city hall, Sullivan turned his combative ambitions toward an old target from his battles at the town financial meetings: the School Department. At this time, the school expenditures were about one-third of the entire city budget. School expenses increased primarily because the number of children in the school system grew as the population rose. Keen on having city hall gain greater control over the school department's finances, Sullivan declared that "the finances of the School Department are absolutely and entirely under the control of the city council." He sharply disagreed with the school committee's view "that the only function of the City Council with respect to the finances of the School Department was that of appropriating the money required for its support in a lump sum to be distributed as the School Committee saw fit."[4] As a result, in its budget, the city council actually set forth the salaries for school administrators and teachers. The school committee ignored these constraints.

Eventually, the dispute reached the Rhode Island Supreme Court, and the court found in favor of the school committee on the basis that since the school committee had the power to hire, it should also have the power to fix salaries; otherwise, there would be "many opportunities for friction and disagreement" between the school committee and the municipal government.[5] Seven decades later, in 1985, the Rhode Island Supreme Court would recall this old case in support of its seminal decision requiring a town council to fund a school contract, even though it would lead to a deficit.[6] Although this decision in 1914 was made to avoid "friction and disagreement," it merely served as the first skirmish in an ongoing battle between school committees and town/city governments in Rhode Island over the control of school finances that continues to this day.

As time passed, voters' anger cooled over how their form of government had been changed. Economic growth spurred population growth in the city, leading to the demand for more government services. Voters now began clamoring for the level of municipal services provided by the City of Providence, such as "a sewerage system, a paid fire department, a higher salaried school teaching staff." Sullivan defended the amount of money the city gave to the School Department by indicating that the "persistent demand on the part of teachers for a raising of the standard of salaries" could not be achieved without a tax increase. As for roads, Sullivan explained that while "every citizen in the city wants to have the street in front of his property improved…there is not money enough available to do it." This growing public dissatisfaction, along with what his critics called "tyrannical" behavior, nearly led to Sullivan's defeat in the mayoral election of 1912, when Sullivan defeated the Republican candidate John W. Horton by only 11 votes—1,892 to 1,881—the closest margin in a mayoral election in Cranston history.

Close elections tend to expose the flaws in our electoral system, and the 1912 Cranston mayoral election exposed voter fraud. Eventually, the Rhode Island Supreme Court resolved the legal dispute by finding that although there had been illegal votes cast in the election, both sides had benefited from the illegal voting; thus, even discounting all the illegal votes, Sullivan was still the winner by at least three votes, but by no more than seven votes. Accordingly, Sullivan remained mayor for another year but had to endeavor to fend off what he deemed to be "malicious misrepresentations and insults." While defending himself from these insults, Sullivan was quick to insult his opponents by calling state legislators "bum legislators" who were "degenerate" and "incompetent."[7]

Sullivan had defeated Horton in Cranston's annual mayoral elections of 1911 and 1912. In the 1913 mayoral election, Sullivan would meet Horton for a third time, but this time it would end differently. Horton called for a "cleaner city" and alleged the existence of a number of illegal barrooms operating within walking distance of city hall. Horton blamed the situation on lax law enforcement by the police department under Sullivan's control. Although Sullivan denied the charges, Horton defeated Sullivan by the clear margin of 53 percent to 45 percent.

Although still a young man at the time he left the mayor's office, Sullivan would never reach the heights of the political success he had once enjoyed. While he attracted controversy and grabbed headlines, he found little electoral success. He would run for mayor five more times, but always unsuccessfully. He would run for governor and mayor at the same time in 1920, losing both offices by landslides. He would run for United States senator in 1924 as an Independent candidate and lose, finishing behind a socialist candidate. His "disdain" for "machine politics" led to personal feuding with leaders in his own Democratic party. Sullivan's personal traits led his critics to call him a "czar" while he was mayor, and it was those same traits that made it difficult for Sullivan to work with others "who seek to advance the same political ideals" after he left the mayor's office.[8]

As he reached old age, Sullivan remained active in public life and would win public office one last time in 1940, elected to the city council, but this time as a Republican.[9] However, he would not complete his term, for he passed way in March 1942. Because of his aversion to debt and tax increases, he did not spend funds liberally to erect buildings, playgrounds or parks, so his name will not be found on public edifices. Instead, the monument he left Cranston was the example of his fiscal policies, which demonstrated "his conviction that good government is a matter of good financing."[10]

JOHN W. HORTON

1914–1922

Public acclaim was not a lifelong ambition of John W. Horton. Born in New Hampshire during the Civil War, Horton spent his early youth working on the family farm while attending school during winter months. Becoming dissatisfied with schooling, he worked in a local hardware store, but the confines of a small country store proved too restricting for Horton, so he became a traveling salesman for a New York company. Eventually, he formed an iron pipes and fittings company and established this company in Cranston, which at the time was growing economically and providing a welcoming business environment for entrepreneurs. After enjoying a lifetime of entrepreneurial success, Horton decided to enter public life by running as the Republican nominee for mayor in 1911. His lack of government experience proved a positive since he was not tainted with any involvement with the change in Cranston's form of government orchestrated by the Republicans. Although unsuccessful in his first two attempts at the mayor's office, eventually Horton won the office of mayor in 1913, on his third attempt, demonstrating that perseverance, for some, will be rewarded.

Horton would need this perseverance through his first year as mayor because of the lingering bitterness from the mayoral campaign of 1913 surrounding the police department. The city council was divided evenly between Democrats and Republicans. Although as mayor, Horton could break a tie vote of the city council, one Republican often broke with his party and joined with the Democrats on key votes. As a result, Horton's nominees for police chief and other positions in the police department were rejected by the city council, while city positions appointed by the city council, such as city auditor and city solicitor, were retained by appointees of the prior Democrat-controlled city council. The rejection of Horton's nominee for police chief was soon followed by the city council's attempt to strip Horton of his powers to appoint the members of the police department.[11] Horton responded by promptly vetoing these ordinances. After a controversial change in its form of government in 1910, and a subsequent rocky transfer of power, Cranston now had to experience a thoroughly divided government.

Unable to exercise the limited powers of appointment granted to him under the charter due to the obstructionism of the city council, Horton used the remaining power given him by the charter—the veto—to thwart the city council on several occasions. Horton vetoed numerous ordinances and resolutions addressing road improvements, street lighting and even poultry and exercised his line-item veto to eliminate funding for the city hall janitor/night watchman. This political melodrama would see its final act in November 1914, when Horton faced Sullivan once again in the mayoral contest, but this time the winner would serve a two-year term. Tired of the turmoil and seeking some stability, the voters reelected Horton by the wide margin of 57 percent to 41 percent and, just as importantly for Horton, gave Republicans control of the city council by a lopsided thirteen-to-three margin.[12] Horton would never face a hostile city council again, and in fact, after the 1916 election, no Democrat would have a seat on the city council until the Great Depression.

The clear reversal in Cranston's political landscape would be reflected in a change in Cranston's fiscal policies. Like the Republicans who dominated Cranston prior to Sullivan, Horton and the Republican city council focused on increasing municipal services to make Cranston an attractive place for homeowners. While Horton called for efficiency in public expenditures and helped establish the predecessor to the Board of Contract and Purchase, he did not consider it "economy to refuse to expend money for needed development." At the start of his term as mayor in 1914, Horton foresaw that Cranston would, "in the near future," confront the problems "familiar to big cities."[13] As a result, Horton expanded government services and expenditures.

In the area of public safety, Horton recommended more police and fire protection. As a result, the police department's staff grew by a third, from a

Growth

staff of twelve full-time employees in 1913 to eighteen full-time employees in 1921. A more conspicuous change occurred in fire protection as Cranston began the gradual shift from all volunteer fire departments, where average citizens came to the rescue of their neighbors for no pay, to a permanent fire department, consisting of well-paid, well-staffed, full-time government employees. In 1921, a permanent fire department was established in Cranston, with a fire station on Pontiac Avenue that was staffed with three full-time employees. At this early date, the cost of this permanent fire department far exceeded the costs to the city for all the volunteer fire departments combined.[14]

However, the most prominent increase in city services occurred in the School Department. During his mayoral campaigns, Horton promised "liberal support of our public schools."[15] To Horton, the school department constituted "one of the most important departments of our municipal government," and more government funding for education was demonstrative of a "progressive and up-to-date attitude." As a result, he justified how, "under the town form of government, Cranston was very

Mayor Horton provided liberal support for public education. After his death, a new elementary school was named in his honor in 1923. It closed in 2006.

liberal in its appropriations for schools and school buildings" and criticized Cranston's prior administration for not keeping "pace with the progress shown by other sections in Rhode Island and elsewhere, in the development of the public school system." Specifically, Horton sought to "at least keep pace with other communities in the matter of the salaries paid to our teachers."[16] As a result, under Horton, school spending tripled in less than decade, from approximately $83,000 in 1913 to approximately $246,645 in 1921, while the number of elementary schools grew quickly as a result of an increasing student population.

At first, Horton was able to avoid increasing property taxes to pay for these increases in government spending because of a fast-growing tax base caused, in part, by new industrial enterprises locating in Cranston. For instance, Universal Winding Company and United Wire and Supply moved to Cranston from Providence in 1914 in order to take advantage of a ten-year tax exemption offered by the City of Cranston for new manufacturers. However, a growing population demanding more government services, along with the high inflation arising from the First World War, necessitated four property tax increases, as the tax rate rose from $1.30 per $100 in 1913 to $2.00 per $100 by 1922. It seems the voters believed these tax increases were acceptable and the increase in government services justified because Horton was reelected mayor by consistently clear margins in 1916, 1918 and 1920.

In his final years in office, Horton began to tackle one of the largest problems facing Cranston as it grew into a city: the need for a sewer system.

Universal Winding Company moved to Cranston in 1914 to take advantage of lower taxes. Renamed Leesona, it moved because of rising taxes and lack of space for expansion. *Courtesy of Cranston Historical Society.*

Growth

In 1921, Horton created a sewer commission to study constructing a sewer system for Cranston and sought $1 million in bonding authority to begin paying for this sewer system. Horton would not live to see work begin on a sewer system. In April 1922, Horton, the avid outdoorsman, died of heart failure while on a fishing trip far away from the troubles and complexities of city life with which he was grappling as mayor.

Horton, the "self-made man," helped remake Cranston by having the city begin to provide the level of services most of us today have come to expect.[17] Although Horton had little formal education, he saw value in education and committed the city to generously funding the Cranston school system. After his death, his commitment to education was recognized when a new primary school was named in his honor. But the honors mortals bestow are not for eternity. The Horton Elementary School would remain open for less than a century. It was closed in 2006 during a less prosperous time, when the City of Cranston was being less forthcoming with funds for its schools and student enrollment was in decline.

ARTHUR A. RHODES

1922–1929

Upon the death of Mayor Horton, Arthur A. Rhodes, the city council president, assumed the office of mayor. Although Rhodes became mayor unexpectedly, he was well prepared for the office. Besides being trained as a lawyer, he and his two brothers managed the popular recreational complex in Pawtuxet that was established by their father. After a devastating fire to the complex, Rhodes and his brothers built Rhodes-on-the-Pawtuxet, a spacious ballroom, which opened in 1915 to a crowd of ten thousand.[18]

In addition to his success in private enterprise, Rhodes held public office for a decade prior to becoming mayor by serving on the city council since 1912 and being the city council president since 1919. As city council president, Rhodes played an important role in the adoption of many of the policies commenced under Horton to have Cranston provide a greater level of municipal services. As mayor, Rhodes would not just continue to increase the level of city services begun under Horton, but he would also try to build on them through public construction on a grand scale.

Before Rhodes could move forward with his building plans, he needed to be elected mayor in his own right. The 1922 mayoral contest pitted Rhodes, as the Republican nominee, against a former city auditor who served in the Sullivan administration. As a result, the election was framed as a choice between the more austere fiscal polices of the Sullivan administration, which focused on lower taxes, and the higher spending policies of the Horton administration, which focused on providing more city services. Although the Democrats won the governorship and made huge gains in the Rhode Island General Assembly because of the decision by Republican governor Emery San Souci to mobilize the National Guard in response to a violent textile strike, Cranston proved itself steadfastly Republican, and Rhodes won with over 60 percent of the vote.[19]

Having claimed the mayoral office despite an unfavorable political climate for his party, Rhodes was emboldened to undertake a new building program to reshape Cranston. At his inauguration in 1923, Rhodes called for a new and larger city hall to be built in the Auburn section, near the newly built fire station and the existing high school, so as to create a civic center for the growing city.[20] However, the price tag of $300,000 for the new city hall building created discontent among those who saw it as an expensive luxury for politicians and others who thought the money would be better spent on schools and highways. It would take a veto by Democratic governor William Flynn on a bill authorizing the city to obtain bonding authority to build this new city hall to stop Rhodes's plans.

Checked in his ambitions to build a new city hall, Rhodes turned to building a sewer system, a recurring issue in Cranston. Although a sewer system was demanded by the most developed sections of Cranston, principally in Edgewood, Rhodes's home ward and a Republican stronghold, its colossal cost, projected to be in the millions, made many voters leery of building one.[21] The opposition to building a sewer system was led by former Mayor Sullivan, the perennial thorn in the side of Cranston's Republican establishment. The high cost of building a sewer system, the reality that all of Cranston would pay for it while the more developed sections of the city would primarily benefit from it and the apparent perception that funds were needed for schools and roads led to the resounding defeat of the sewer bond

Growth

by a two-to-one margin in a referendum held in November 1923. The failure of Cranston to have a sewer system during the 1920s led some disgruntled Edgewood residents to support the annexation of Edgewood by the city of Providence, but these annexation efforts were as unsuccessful as their efforts to obtain sewer service during this decade.

Facing intense public opposition to his building schemes, as well as scathing attacks for having his annual mayoral salary more than tripled from $1,000 to $3,500, Rhodes adapted to these new circumstances and channeled his building ambitions to areas where he would find more public support. Instead of a new city hall for public officials, or an expensive sewer system to benefit the more developed sections of the community, Rhodes called for "good schools, good roads and a sense of security and protection."[22] For roads, Rhodes obtained bonding authority and increased the annual budget expense for improvements from approximately $30,000 a year to well over $100,000 in some years. For schools, Rhodes substantially increased the city's funding from $270,000 to $445,000 from 1922 to 1929 and supported a wave of new school construction, including the building of a new Cranston High School at the cost of approximately $750,000.

The real estate boom of the 1920s led to the construction of Cranston High School, now renamed Cranston High School East.

Not only did Rhodes spend more money on roads and schools, but he also spent more on fire and police protection. It was only a generation earlier, in 1891, that Cranston's first volunteer fire company had been organized. However, once a full-time fire department had been established in 1921 at Pontiac Avenue, it was only a matter of time before residents in other sections of Cranston demanded a fire station located in their neighborhoods, staffed with full-time employees. Apparently, the service from a nearby volunteer fire company appeared inadequate once residents began paying taxes for a full-time fire station in another part of the community. Rhodes rapidly built new fire stations for the expanding full-time fire department. A fire station in Arlington at the Cranston Print Works and then a fire station in Edgewood were quickly built, with the cost of the fire department increasing dramatically for the city from $10,000 to nearly $80,000 per year. In addition, from 1922 to 1929, the full-time police staff nearly doubled from eighteen to thirty-three.

Lastly, the mayor, whose family had made its name and its fortune from providing recreational entertainment to the public, urged the city council to focus on furnishing recreational facilities for the city's youth. In 1928, he finally succeeded in having a new athletic field, located at the Narragansett speedway, built at a cost of $30,000. With a new high school, a new athletic field, two new fire stations and various road improvements, the city was now providing many of the amenities of city life in a suburban community.

Not surprisingly, with all this construction, the city's budget crossed the $1 million level for the first time in 1926 and, in fact, more than doubled under Rhodes. However, Rhodes only raised taxes once as mayor, from $2.00 to $2.15 per $100, which was necessary to fund the building of the new high school. Rhodes was able to increase spending to pay for this new public construction and increase city services because of the growth in the city's tax base as a result of a massive residential real estate boom in the 1920s that made Cranston into a "fairy land of real estate values," where "new dwellings sprung into being almost overnight."[23] This building boom was partly the result of Cranston's adoption, in 1924, of a zoning plan, which ensured that Cranston would become a "city of homes." The focus of this zoning plan was to make Cranston "primarily a residential suburb" in which homeownership would be "promoted," where industry would be kept "subordinate" and where homeowners would be "protected from the encroachment of three deckers and larger tenements" that dominated Providence.[24] As a result, during the 1920s, more middle-class families moved to Cranston, causing its population to grow from 29,407 to 42,911, while Providence's population declined for the first time. This fortuitous real

Growth

Rhodes-on-the-Pawtuxet, a spacious ballroom, opened in 1915. In the early 1990s, it barely avoided demolition.

estate boom made Rhodes a very popular politician. He would be called "Cranston's prosperity mayor," and he was reelected to the mayor's office in 1924 and 1926 with more than 70 percent of the vote, a feat no other mayor of Cranston would surpass for over half a century.[25]

According to the old English proverb, "all good things must come to an end," and so it came to pass. The prosperity of the 1920s proved to be a mere fairy tale without a fairy tale ending. The real estate boom was followed by a real estate bust. Rhodes's time in politics would abruptly end when he decided not to seek reelection as mayor in order to manage Rhodes-on-the-Pawtuxet after the sudden death of his brother in the summer of 1928.[26] Rhodes's own death occurred in 1944, when the big bands were in their heyday and Rhodes-on-the-Pawtuxet was in its glory. But, like all things human, popular musical tastes are not immutable. After going into a period of decline, the wondrous Rhodes-on-the-Pawtuxet barely avoided demolition about a half century after the death of its ambitious builder.

Frank C. Speck

1929–1931

Frank C. Speck's tenure as mayor did not benefit from the booming prosperity of the 1920s but rather coincided with the beginning of the Great Depression. Born in New Jersey, Speck had managed a shirt factory in that state before he came to Cranston in the early twentieth century in order to oversee the shirt factory at the Rhode Island State Prison. Eventually, he managed a shirt factory in Auburn and was one of the first members of Cranston's businessmen's association.

Speck first entered politics by being elected to the Cranston City Council in 1920 and served for six years, two as city council president, an office he obtained by a single vote after a bitter split within the Cranston Republican Party in which he and Mayor Rhodes were on opposite sides. After serving two years in the state senate, Speck became the Republican nominee for mayor in 1928. The 1928 mayoral election occurred in the midst of a historic presidential election in which Governor Al Smith campaigned as the Democratic presidential nominee, the first time a Roman Catholic was the presidential nominee of a major party. This caused an upsurge in Democratic support in heavily Catholic Rhode Island, but the growing political strength of Catholics also led to a backlash in the form of increased activity by the Ku Klux Klan in Rhode Island.

In addition, the controversial issue of building a sewer system resurfaced in Cranston when a proposal to build a $2.5 million sewer system was put on the ballot for voter approval. As a result, the Democrats nominated former Mayor Sullivan, who had made opposition to a city sewer system his cause célèbre. Although support for Smith was strong in some parts of Cranston, he lost Cranston by a two-to-one margin while carrying Rhode Island by a slim margin. As for the sewer plan, it was rejected by a clear margin, and Cranston remained one of only two cities of its size in the nation without a sewer system.[27] For Speck, the results were a close call. Speck won with only

52 percent of the vote and lost three of Cranston's four wards, including his home ward. He was only able to defeat Sullivan by relying on a landslide vote from the First Ward, which was heavily Republican and the only ward to have voted in favor of the sewer plan.

Concerned by the mounting city debt in recent years, Mayor Speck wanted to slow down the increase in government services in Cranston. For example, Speck, a former president of a volunteer fire company, opposed further expansion of the fire department and in fact argued that a "slower development" of the city fire department, which was already more expensive and had a larger staff than the police department, was a better approach.[28] Also, Speck exhibited farsightedness when he wisely observed that the additional property tax revenue gained from more residential developments is eventually exceeded by the cost to the city of providing additional city services for these new homeowners.[29] By adopting a zoning policy in 1924 that primarily promoted residential development, Cranston would become a "city of homes," but it would also become a city where its level of municipal services grew faster than its tax base. As a result, in 1929, the property tax rate was increased from $2.15 to $2.30 per $100.

Speck's more cautious view of development was also reflected in his approach to additional public construction in Cranston. Under Speck's tenure, there was little new public construction in Cranston, with the exception of the establishment of a playground in each of the city's four wards and the completion of an additional elementary school.

Rather than a real estate boom or new public buildings, Speck's brief tenure as mayor would be noted for controversy. Because of the vast increase in city spending, Speck saw the need for more oversight, so he recommended more auditing of the city's finances and "rigid economy."[30] His increased oversight led to the discovery that a two-year garbage collection contract, which had begun in 1927 under his predecessor, Rhodes, had resulted in the contractor being overpaid each month, so instead of paying the contractor $7,400 a year, the city was paying this contractor $9,900 a year.[31] Here was an early instance of where the mistakes of a prior administration can eventually bring troubles to a future one. Unfortunately, Speck compounded the error. Instead of refusing to make the last two monthly payments under the contract to rectify the error, Speck made these last two payments fearing that the contractor would refuse to collect the trash and the error would need to be disclosed to the public.[32] But a coverup does not make the original mistake go away, it only makes it worse.

A year later, in 1930, the overpayment was disclosed, and the garbage contractor accused Speck of accepting a $1,500 bribe from the contractor's son to cover up the overpayment. Speck denied the charges. It was soon discovered that the garbage contractor's son had taken the $1,500 from his father, not for a bribe, but for his own personal use, and that the bribery accusation itself had been made with the help of the contractor's son-in-law, who was a member of the Cranston Democratic party, so the charge of bribery lacked any credibility.[33] Legal proceedings by the city commenced shortly thereafter against the contractor for reimbursement of the overpayment, and the city prevailed. Eventually, the city council investigated the matter and found no justifiable excuse for any of the overpayments; it blamed the blunder on Speck, Rhodes and other city financial officials.[34] In the end, Speck would have to admit that he should not have made the last two overpayments and could only lament, "Can a man do more than admit publically that he has made a mistake, an honest mistake of judgment?"[35]

Having learned that the life of a public official "is not a smooth and pleasant one" and that his hard work and his good deeds were taken for granted while "one small miscalculation" could lead to much torment, the elderly Speck decided not to seek reelection in October 1930 after serving only one term.[36] Nearly three years later, in 1933, his life journey would come to an end when Speck collapsed and died on a hot summer day shortly after returning home from a business trip.

Frederick A. Jones

1931–1935

Although Speck departed from the mayor's office, the gloom of the Great Depression did not depart from Cranston, but only deepened, and Mayor Frederick A. Jones would have to lead Cranston through its lowest depths. Born in Wisconsin, he came to Rhode Island to obtain an education at Brown University and stayed when he found a growing state economy. Jones became a corporate lawyer and served on the boards of various local businesses, including United Wire and

Supply, a manufacturer and one of Cranston's largest employers. He held various elected offices: city council, school committee and senator, but only briefly. To him, public service was a civic duty but not a profession. With the last-minute decision by Mayor Speck not to seek reelection, Republican Party leaders convinced a reluctant Jones to run for mayor in 1930. Although he had not run for office in over decade, Jones won with a decisive 56 percent of the vote over former Mayor Sullivan and carried three of Cranston's five wards, while the Republicans captured every seat on the city council except for those elected by the new Fifth Ward.

During the Great Depression, some wanted the government to intervene economically and to experiment with new approaches, but Jones was not one of them. Instead, starting with his first inaugural address, Jones sought to "revive the old-fashioned virtue of economy." He would preach this message throughout his tenure as mayor, from inaugural addresses and speeches before taxpayer associations and the chamber of commerce to radio addresses for the public directly. Jones believed that city governments, by expanding their services, were "trying to give too much government." He said that the "great increase in the number of municipal activities" was unnecessary and that "adding new activities and greatly expanding old ones" made little sense if the city "cannot pay" for "fundamental municipal activities." This demonstrates that the sentiment that there is "too much government" has long existed in political discourse. Jones theorized that the "extravagance of individuals" had "affected" the city's "municipal finance ideals," and since "as individuals, we have been spending as never before," and with it "individual thrift and economy has lessened," so had government spending increased while government economy had decreased. This observation could easily be made of consumer behavior and government spending habits in recent decades.

Sagely understanding that voters had a "dual and inconsistent attitude" about taxation and spending, Jones realized that voters "cry aloud that taxes are too high and must be reduced, and the next day lend active support to some new activity which will cost the city" more money. He noted that "no great increase in our expenditures is made without some aggressive demand on the part of the voters." Accordingly, Jones comprehended that voters "are all in favor of reduced taxes so long as curtailment" in government spending "does not affect" them "directly."[37] Keen observers of current public opinion would find little to disagree with Jones's conclusions.

More remarkable is that Jones not only preached the message of "greater conservatism" but also actually practiced it. For example, in 1932, the worst year of the Great Depression, he had the city council and the Cranston

School Committee unilaterally cut salaries of all their employees by 10 percent. Although Jones did not face organized opposition to these cuts from organized labor, since the right to collectively bargain for government employees was only bestowed on public employees three decades later by the Rhode Island General Assembly, Jones was still criticized for it. However, the public applauded his efforts and cheered his success at maintaining a balanced budget while reducing the debt and not raising taxes.[38] As a result, Jones won reelection in 1932 with 64 percent of the vote and carried every ward, including the heavily Democratic Fifth Ward.

Even after Franklin Roosevelt became president and started the New Deal, which led the federal government to initiate a large public works program, Jones still opposed increasing government spending on borrowed money. Jones believed that Cranston "had spent vastly more than we could afford" and that Cranston was already "trying to do too much" of its "business on extended credit." Instead of "public works almost wholly built with borrowed money," he believed that "conservative management" was of greater importance "than any public works program which the Mayor can suggest."[39] As a result, he advised against the building of a new city hall while the Great Depression was ongoing. This eventually resulted in a dramatic confrontation between Jones and his own Republican-controlled city council.

When Roosevelt's Public Works Administration began offering federal funds for public works projects, the temptation of a large pot of federal money with which to award government contracts and dole out jobs was too much for some in Jones's party, and they seized it as an opportunity to finally build a new city hall. Jones argued that that a "reduction of taxes" was "more necessary at the present time than a new City Hall." He noted that the federal government was not paying the entire cost of various public works projects, but instead the city would need to pay at least half of the expense. But in politics, economic arguments often carry no weight when patronage is at stake.

The city council passed, even over the veto of Jones, a resolution to build a new city hall and ignored the recommendation of the City Planning Commission of where to build it. Former Mayor Sullivan, who had lost to Jones in 1930, came to Jones's support and threatened to circulate a petition seeking the resignation of every councilman who voted to override Jones's veto. However, after the city council overrode the mayor's veto, Jones refused to sign the application for federal funds for the new city hall. While city council members began asking for legal opinions, Mayor

Jones calmly stated that he was "more concerned in expressing wishes for a prosperous and happy New Year" to Cranston residents.[40] The new city hall project languished until a very different mayoral administration entered office in 1935.

Despite angering leaders in his own party over the issue of building a new city hall, Jones remained popular. Numerous attempts by some in his party were made to persuade Jones to seek renomination, and the Democratic Party indicated that it would endorse him and thereby make his reelection to mayor "almost unanimous."[41] However, Jones declined renomination as mayor in 1934. He had fulfilled his civic obligation and wanted to return to private life. Jones went back to his corporate law practice, where he diligently served his clients until he died while working at his desk in 1941.

The extraordinary in history does not only occur through the achievements of a celebrated figure on a large, illuminated stage. Sometimes it happens far away from where our attention is focused, through the efforts of a less well-known, quieter individual. Roosevelt, with his eloquence, charm and dexterous political skills, changed the course of our nation's history and became a popular political figure by advocating for a New Deal. At the same time, Jones followed an entirely different path and became incredibly popular in Cranston by simply following the old-fashioned virtue of thrift. Even after slashing the salaries of public employees and refusing to undertake a major public works project that would have been federally subsidized, Jones remained so popular that he could have been reelected as mayor without opposition in the midst of the nation's greatest economic crisis. This alone must rank as something rather extraordinary, or at least noteworthy and deserving of being remembered. Although Jones did not change Cranston's trajectory, it was not because his traditional views on spending were without merit but because his successors did not, for various reasons, find it expedient to follow Jones's venerable principles.

Transformation

1935–1960

Ernest L. Sprague

1935–1943

Serving in government was more than a temporary duty for Ernest L. Sprague; it was his life. Sprague was born in 1872, a year before the Panic of 1873, which brought on the demise of the financial empire of his distant kinsmen, the Spragues of Cranston. At a young age, Sprague began working for the Rhode Island General Assembly and subsequently obtained a clerical position with the Rhode Island secretary of state. With the resignation of the secretary of state because of illness, he was elected by the Rhode Island General Assembly to serve as the Rhode Island secretary of state in January 1924. The voters elected and reelected him to this office until 1932, when Republicans lost in a historic election. After working in government for nearly four decades, a single electoral defeat would not deter Sprague's political ambitions. Sprague became chairman of the Rhode Island Republican Party at a time when party leaders were still powerful and the Republican Party was still a power in Rhode Island. When Cranston Republicans needed a mayoral candidate in 1934, Sprague seized the opportunity and won with approximately 60 percent of the vote.

Although Sprague spoke of carrying on his predecessors' policies, he quickly reversed the course set by his immediate predecessor. Sprague called for the building of a new city hall because the existing one in Knightsville was a "fire hazard" and failing to build a new city hall would show a "lack of civic pride."[1] Within a few months of taking office, Sprague had secured a federal grant from the Public Works Administration to build a new city hall. Once federal funding was secured, a bitter battle ensued over where to locate the new city hall. The City Planning Commission had recommended that a new city hall be built in Oaklawn. The Democrats wanted it to remain in Knightsville. The Republicans wanted it located in Auburn. The school committee opposed construction next to the newly built high school. The Rhode Island House of Representatives, which was under Democratic control, passed legislation requiring a referendum on locating the new city hall, but the bill stalled in the Republican-controlled senate.

When some members of the city council wanted more time to study the location of city hall, Sprague, fearing that delay could imperil federal funding for the project, demanded speedy action and engaged in what his critics called "steamroller tactics," resulting in a city council vote to build the new city hall on Park Avenue.[2] His tactics may have angered some, but the end result made him popular. Sprague won reelection in 1936 by a landslide. The cornerstone for the new city hall was laid in December 1936, and on May 12, 1937, the building of the new city hall was completed at a cost of $270,000, with the federal government funding approximately $121,500. Despite much "bickering and quarrelling," one newspaper called the opening of the new city hall "an eventful day in Cranston history."[3] It could also have been called a symbolic day for Cranston and a turning point in its history.

With the construction of a new city hall, Sprague urged an increase in public employee compensation. Sprague, the life-long public employee, wanted to reverse the 10 percent salary cut that city and school employees had received in 1932 and to begin granting automatic salary increases to these employees. In addition to salary increases, Sprague wanted to provide the new fringe benefit of pensions to police officers. Sprague noted that other Rhode Island cities were providing pensions to their police officers, while

Transformation

With federal funding, Cranston City Hall was built in 1937, despite the opposition of Mayor Jones, who preferred to lower taxes, and partisan battles regarding its location.

others pointed to the recent enactment of Social Security and the existence of pension plans in private industry. Although the city had experienced a recent budget deficit from rapid growth in the cost of unemployment assistance from $197,545 in 1935 to $334,374 in 1937, the city council followed Sprague's recommendations, restoring one-half of the 10 percent pay cut to all city and school employees in 1937, and the other half in 1941. In addition, Cranston obtained enabling legislation from the Rhode Island General Assembly to create a police pension fund, which allowed police officers to retire at any age after twenty-five years of service with a pension at 50 percent of the average pay they had received during their last five years of service. The pension was originally funded by two contributions of $5,000, one from the city and the other from the police association. Police officers would be required to contribute only 1 percent of their salaries to the pension fund.

Within a year of the pension fund being established, the first police officer retired. Sprague had promised voters that the pension fund would be "self-sustaining,"[4] but he created it with no actuarial studies and funded it with only a 1 percent deduction from police officers' salaries. Unwittingly, Sprague set Cranston on a long, tortured journey involving unfunded pension liabilities. It was a path that others had just begun. In 1935, the federal government set foot on this path with the passage of Social Security for private sector workers. In 1936, the state government of Rhode Island would follow by creating a pension plan for state employees. In 1937, Cranston would make the fateful turn down this road.

The increasing burden of providing unemployment relief, which fell heavily on cities and towns, caused Sprague to call on the state government to levy new taxes and share the new tax revenues with cities and towns. This kind of solution would be heard from time to time from the municipal officials of troubled communities for many years to come. While the State of Rhode Island was limited in the amount of new revenues it could provide to Cranston, the federal government was hiring the unemployed for various public works projects under Roosevelt's Works Progress Administration (WPA). Under Sprague, Cranston took full advantage of federal assistance for public works projects. For example, during Sprague's mayoral tenure, many of Cranston's sidewalks were built with WPA funds. Also, Cranston turned its recreation field into Cranston Stadium with the hope that it would attract major sporting events, although Sprague's critics ridiculed it as an expensive replica of a Roman amphitheatre. In addition, in 1938, Cranston built Budlong Pool, one of the largest outdoor swimming pools in the nation, but its opening was delayed because the city had not budgeted for a field house to be used by swimmers for dressing. After city hall was "stormed" by protesting children in 1939, the field house was built and the pool briefly opened in 1940. However, concerns of the State Board of Health caused the pool to be open only on a temporary basis in 1941, and for a time it appeared that the pool would have to be "practically rebuilt" for it to reopen. These miscalculations led one newspaper editorial to label the Budlong Pool "an embarrassing white elephant," while one Cranston public official admitted it was a "complete flop."[5] Eventually, in the summer of 1942, the Budlong Pool finally opened on a regular basis after a permit was issued by another state agency.

The most anticipated and most controversial public works project in Cranston history was the sewer project. Since Cranston had become a city, the issue of building a sewer system had been debated many times, and proposals to build one had been rejected twice by the voters in 1923 and 1928. However, with the federal government providing funding for public works projects, some anticipated that it was now time to build a sewer system. Believing that federal funds from the WPA would be forthcoming, Sprague sought legislation from the Rhode Island General Assembly to seek voter approval for a sewer bond. But on the last night of the legislative session, the bill died in the House of Representatives when Republicans would not agree to a deal to give prominent Democratic representative Walter Sepe control over a seat on the commission overseeing the sewer project.[6]

Political power soon shifted with the election in 1938, when Republicans regained control of the Rhode Island General Assembly and the governorship. After being reelected again, Sprague announced that he would seek legislation to grant Cranston the authority to issue a sewer bond of $2.5 million. The proposed legislation was criticized because the sewer bonds would not need voter approval and could be repaid through taxation of all residents, although some neighborhoods would not receive sewer service. Although Cranston voters had twice rejected authorization to build a sewer system, Sprague defended the lack of a voter referendum by arguing that it was unnecessary, since city officials supported the project and speed was needed to secure federal funding. As to the possibility of taxing non-sewer users for the sewer system, Sprague promised, "Nobody will be asked to share in the paying for sewers unless he is afforded the privilege of using them."[7] The allure of federal money proved too enticing. The General Assembly quickly and unanimously passed the bill, and Governor William Vanderbilt promptly signed it.

The Sewer Act of 1939 aroused extreme euphoria and exaggeration in Cranston. It was anticipated that the sewer project would be an engine of economic growth by reducing unemployment, attracting new businesses and raising home property values. The act was heralded as "Cranston's Declaration of Independence."[8] In fact, Sprague treated the pen with which the governor signed the bill into law with some reverence when he presented it to the city council, which solemnly accepted the pen as a gift to be kept at city hall. When sewer construction began on June 3, 1939, a speaker at the dedication ceremony called for a day of "Thanksgiving."[9]

The Cranston sewer project was "the greatest sewer project ever undertaken by WPA labor."[10] But, there were early signs that this project would prove to be beyond the ability of the WPA. In 1940, the WPA began providing fewer workers than promised, and these workers were very unskilled. As a result, Cranston had to begin taking out short-term loans to pay for other laborers to perform the sewer construction. Walter Sepe, now a city councilman, warned that Cranston was on the "verge of bankruptcy" and that the sewer project would cost millions more than originally promised.[11] However, his warnings were ignored. Sprague and Cranston's Republicans would ride a wave of enthusiasm over the sewer project to total victory in 1940, when Sprague won by a landslide once again,

With assistance from the federal WPA, it was anticipated that the Cranston sewer project would be an engine of economic growth. The fanfare surrounding the sewer project faded as the costs rose.

this time winning for the first time the heavily Democratic Fifth Ward and seeing every seat on the city council captured by a Republican.

Only from the highest of heights do the greatest of falls occur. Slowly, the fanfare surrounding the sewer project faded as the costs rose and the troubles became more apparent. At first, the sewer project was expected to be completed in 1941 at a cost of $6 million, of which the city would pay only $2.5 million; the other $3.5 million would be provided by the federal government through the WPA.[12] It was "only" because of federal funds that Sprague had gone forward with the sewer project.[13] However, WPA labor was "neither [as] experienced nor [as] efficient" as "experienced contractors and laborers."[14] In addition, as the American economy shifted toward war production, a "shortage of men on WPA rolls" became apparent, and the expected contribution from the federal government in the form of WPA labor fell as the Second World War progressed. Work on the sewer project began stalling and falling behind schedule. This lack of WPA labor not only caused delays but also meant the federal government contributed less to the project while Cranston's share of the project's costs grew more. Along with the reduction in federal funding came a rise in the costs of labor and materials as a result of wartime economics. The costs of the sewer project soared from $6 million to $9 million, and the city's share, which was supposed to have been only $2.5 million, reached $5 million in just a few years.[15]

In 1941, there were revelations about "political interference" by city officials in the sewer project. These allegations were made by the chairman of the Cranston Sewer Commission as he resigned his post. In 1942, it was now the turn of the state WPA administrator to accuse Cranston officials of "extravagance and inference" in the sewer project, and WPA involvement was pulled from project.[16] During these two years, there were stories about the hiring of various workers for partisan purposes, the improper charging of expenses to the sewer project by city departments and an admission by Sprague that the original cost estimates for the sewer project were based on "pure guesswork."[17] All of this caused the sewer project to give off quite a stench.

Editorials by different newspapers were quick to condemn the Cranston sewer project. One newspaper called the "whole sewer program" a "gigantic and costly flop" and an "unmitigated calamity" caused by "stupidity, inefficiency, jealously" and "politicking."[18] Another newspaper called the Cranston sewer project "perhaps the most costly piece of municipal bungling in the history of Rhode Island" and blamed it mostly on "politics." The newspaper specifically referred to "the doctoring of cost estimates," which was done to "prevent public protest against the undertaking." It also mentioned how "incompetent workmen" were hired and retained on the sewer project. The newspaper pointed the finger of blame at "a greasy gang of behind-the-scenes politicians" who made a "multi-million dollar fiasco out of what should have been a sound public improvement."[19] The sewer controversy was simply "without parallel in Cranston history."[20]

The "political situation in Cranston" soon slipped "into confusion and hysteria." In this crisis, the Cranston Republican Party saw its most powerful party leader step away from it all. Clarence Mertz, who had been a Cranston Republican Party leader since the days of Mayor Sullivan and had been called its "unofficial party boss" for years, suddenly quit politics.[21] One newspaper called it the "end of era," and it was for Cranston's Republicans. After the sewer debacle, they would never again dominate Cranston politics like they had done for nearly three decades under Mertz.

In politics, gratitude and loyalty have no place if it means not winning on election day. Cranston Republican Party leaders saw that "public opposition" to Sprague could not be "ignored any longer" and that he had "lost the last vestige of public confidence."[22] Sprague tried to save himself by issuing a written defense, but it was a futile attempt, with one newspaper editorial ridiculing it as "lame and pathetic."[23] In the end, Sprague was discarded as the Republican mayoral nominee for 1942 at his party's convention, and his career of holding "political desk jobs" came to a close. A year later, in 1943, the sewer project was halted with only two-thirds complete and millions of dollars over budget. A year after that, in 1944, Sprague's life came to an end.

For a few decades in the nineteenth century, a family of industrialists called the Spragues had dominated Cranston, until the Panic of 1873 drove them into bankruptcy. With their private fortune, they had built a factory and a mansion, both of which still stand as reminders of the family's once formidable wealth and power. For a few years in the twentieth century, a powerful politician, also named Sprague, dominated Cranston politics. With federal funds, he built a city hall, a stadium and one of the nation's largest outdoor pools. But it was the building of the sewer system that lies unseen beneath our feet that brought about his departure from public office. Some believe that there are ghosts that haunt the Sprague Mansion. There have been no sightings of specters at Cranston City Hall, but for years, Sprague's unfinished sewer project would bedevil Cranston officials, and to this day, Sprague's unfunded pension plan haunts Cranston and will do so for decades to come.

William G. Lind

1943–1945

William G. Lind entered politics only after becoming a successful businessman in the jewelry manufacturing industry. Lind served on the city council for eight years, six as president, and was a state representative for six years. He had worked with Mayor Sprague, first as city council president supporting the building of a new city hall and then as a state representative sponsoring enabling legislation that would allow Cranston to establish a pension plan for police officers. With Sprague's popularity plummeting, various

Transformation

Republicans began seeking an alternative and convinced Lind to be a candidate for mayor. Lind was considered the "insurgent" candidate but resented being called such after his long tenure in public office as a staunch Republican. In recent years, Lind had "freely and sharply criticized" the Sprague administration and had become a "critic of machine Republicanism."[24]

Faced with a choice between an unpopular incumbent, Sprague, and an electable insurgent, Lind, party leaders dropped Sprague at the party's local convention in 1942 and backed Lind. However, the sewer controversy had not only divided the Republicans but also weakened their dominance over local politics in Cranston. The Cranston mayoral race in 1942 was a three-way race. Lind won the mayor's office, but with only 45 percent of the vote. The Democratic mayoral candidate garnered 30 percent of the vote and, as expected, won the Fifth Ward. Hoyt W. Lark, a former president of the chamber of commerce running as an Independent, had a surprisingly strong showing by taking 25 percent of the vote and carrying the reliably Republican Second Ward. With a fractured party and a splintered electorate, Lind became mayor.

The immediate problem facing Lind was to clean up the muddled financing of the bungled sewer project. After the passage of new legislation, Lind refinanced $2.5 million of short-term notes used to pay for the sewer construction into longer-term bonds. Next, he had an annual sewer charge assessed on all sewer users, which for the average homeowner was $12 per year. These financial steps addressed the most immediate problems surrounding the sewer project. Later in the summer of 1943, with labor and materials needed for building sewers becoming scarce and too expensive due to the Second World War, the decision was made to stop further construction of the sewer system with the hope that it would resume after the war concluded.

After helping to untangle the snarl of sewer financing, Lind dove into the quagmire of pension funding. After police officers began receiving pension benefits, Lind called for firefighters to receive them as well. This pattern of extending a benefit to one group of public employees after it had been bestowed on another group of public employees would continue throughout Cranston's history. In 1944, Cranston obtained enabling legislation from the Rhode Island General Assembly to create a firefighters' pension plan. The principal proposal before the city council required firefighters to have thirty-five years of service and reach a minimum retirement age of fifty-eight years before they could receive a pension at 50 percent of their average pay over their last five years of service. There was also a dispute as to whether firefighters should contribute 3 percent or 5 percent of their salaries to the pension fund. Firefighters opposed these more stringent pension requirements. These firefighters felt they were "entitled" to a better pension plan and believed that a 5 percent contribution to the pension plan was "exorbitant," although it had been recommended by the actuary.[25] The firefighters demanded a pension after only twenty-five years of service, with no more than a 3 percent contribution. The city council hesitated in creating this new pension fund, since the city had already failed to make any payments into the recently created police pension fund, other than the original city contribution of $5,000.[26] Also, actuarial experts warned city officials that promising pensions without adequately funding them would eventually put a severe financial burden on the city.

While the city council proceeded with caution, Lind called for prompt action and denounced the city council's behavior as mere "stalling tactics."[27] To the cheers of the gallery, Lind spoke of the "greatness of the city's fire department" and promised to work for a "proper reward for the firemen."[28] Although the city council eventually passed an ordinance bestowing pensions on firefighters, the firefighters were dissatisfied with it and believed it was "unfair."[29] The pension plan was not implemented, since the 5 percent salary contribution from firefighters was not included in the enabling legislation passed by the Rhode Island General Assembly. The firefighters would have to wait until the next administration in order to obtain the pension plan to which they thought they were entitled.

Lind left after only serving one term as mayor because of feuds with leaders in his own party. The one-time insurgent mayoral candidate acted as a mayor independent of party leaders. Lind, who opposed "favorites getting jobs or contracts," battled with party leaders over the hiring of a purchasing agent and his appointment of a chairman to the City Planning Commission.[30] At one city council meeting, a dispute arose over the creation of an inspector position in the police department. Under the existing city charter, as mayor, Lind presided over city council meetings and could break a tie vote. But on this occasion, Lind decided to cast a vote in order to create a tie and then used his power as presiding officer to block any attempt to have another vote or allow any request for an opinion from the city solicitor regarding the legality of what was transpiring.[31] At the party convention in 1944, Lind was dumped for Lark, who was now back in the Republican fold. The Republican Party leaders dispensed with the insurgent who acted independently as mayor in favor of the former Independent whom they hoped they could depend on as mayor. Lind, a self-described "political orphan," left office denouncing local Republican Party leaders as "five little men" constituting an "unseen government."[32]

In one of his last speeches as mayor, Lind quipped, "I'll be forgotten, but my picture will be here." Mayor Lind's picture still hangs at Cranston City Hall, and although many who pass by it have forgotten who he was, Lind should be remembered as the first candidate to challenge his own party's leadership and become mayor. Lind said he "enjoyed breaking precedents" and that he did so by openly challenging and momentarily defeating his party's leadership. With Lind began the long transformation in local politics that eventually saw the power of party bosses in Cranston broken. Although his tenure as mayor was brief and difficult, Lind enjoyed a long life and died in 1974 at the age of ninety-two.[33]

Hoyt W. Lark

1945–1953

Although he served as president of the Cranston Chamber of Commerce, Hoyt W. Lark was not a businessman but a Harvard-educated attorney. As president of the chamber of commerce, Lark advocated for having sewer service in Cranston, and when the sewer construction project began in 1939, he was credited by some as being the "man who did the most to bring sewers to Cranston." But when the sewer project he championed turned into an embarrassment, Lark blamed Mayor Sprague's Republican administration. As a result, he ran as an Independent for mayor in 1942, proclaiming, "I am not a politician." He garnered 25 percent of the vote in a three-way race and won the Second Ward. Fearing that his independent candidacy could lead to a Democratic victory and displeased with Mayor Lind's independence, local Republican Party leaders reached an understanding with Lark and his supporters. As a result, Lark became the Republican mayoral nominee in 1944 and won the office with 54 percent of the vote. After changing party affiliation to become mayor, Lark would oversee dramatic changes to Cranston during his mayoral term.[34]

When Lark entered office, he tried to put city financing on a pay-as-you-go basis and tried to stop continued deficit spending. Lark noted that for decades Cranston had used tax anticipation notes to help with cash flow. While Sprague was mayor, the city's operating deficits had soared. For instance, in 1939, the city had to borrow $175,000 to cover its deficit stemming from the increase in public assistance. In 1945, the city had an operating deficit of $739,000, but by 1950, it had been reduced to $240,000. However, this was not accomplished by a reduction in spending.

Because of wartime inflation, there was a sharp rise in the cost of living. As a result, large salary increases for teachers and city employees were approved, which necessitated, in 1945, a property tax increase from $2.30 per hundred to $2.40 per hundred, the first property tax increase in Cranston since 1929. However, salary increases were not the only form of compensation that some city employees demanded. The firefighters insisted on a pension, but when the "over cautious city council" wanted to provide a pension to firefighters who had thirty-five years of service, firefighters expressed their dissatisfaction and pressed for receiving a pension after only twenty-five years of service.[35] Lark tried to explain the difficulty of providing this level of pension benefits on an "actuarial basis," and a city council member noted that the police pension plan was in need of changing because of the cost the city would soon incur for recently retired police officers, but the firefighters were not persuaded.[36]

Eventually, in 1946, Lark acquiesced to the firefighters' demands, and a firefighters' pension plan requiring twenty-five years of service with a minimum age requirement of fifty-five and a 5 percent contribution from firefighters' salaries was approved.[37] Lark would bend even further in 1951, when the minimum age requirement was dropped entirely from the firefighters' pension plan.[38] However, to his credit, Lark tried to properly fund these pension benefits by having the city invest $10,000 per year into the pension system for firefighters and police officers, allowing the city to create reserves from which to pay retirees out of interest income and payroll deductions.

But the agitation by Cranston's government employees for more compensation was only beginning. In 1946, Cranston teachers were so dissatisfied with the amount of their salary increase that some members threatened to strike.[39] In response, the sympathetic Lark called for better pay

Transformation

for all government employees, in particular teachers, whom he believed were "inadequately paid" because education was "the most important thing we have to do."[40] Thus, throughout Lark's mayoral term, both city and school employees would receive repeated salary increases.

Cranston's rapid residential development had been interrupted by economic depression and worldwide conflagration. With the end of the Second World War, building materials became available again, and easy mortgage terms made it affordable for young families to build their own homes in Cranston. Garden City, the state's "most well-known subdivision" and a suburban showcase, began in 1947, leading the way for Cranston's new housing boom.[41] Cranston's population grew from 47,085 in 1940 to 66,766 by 1960. To Lark, this housing boom meant that there would be a boom in the demand for "more schools, more highways, more police and fire protection; in fact, more of everything."[42]

In response, Lark built a new fire station in the Oak Lawn section. Lark also restarted the sewer project, finally bringing sewer service to Edgewood decades after its residents had first sought it. However, this expansion of

After the Second World War, Garden City was at one time a suburban showcase. This housing boom led to the building of Garden City Elementary School.

the sewer system came at the price of $2.5 million. Furthermore, because the cost of the sewer system exceeded the revenues it generated, Cranston implemented a sewer tax on property owners who chose not to be connected to the sewer system. In addition, Lark supported the construction of four new elementary schools, including one in Garden City, and a new middle school at a cost of approximately $4 million. Not only were new facilities built, but also, in eight years, Lark greatly expanded the police and fire departments by increasing their staffing by approximately 50 percent while doubling their budgets.

It was apparent that this rapid increase in government spending could require higher taxes. Although Lark admitted that the city "could take strict economy measures" by reverting to the "old volunteer fire companies" and replacing "many permanent police officers with constables," Lark was not about to have Cranston become "a one-horse town." For Lark, if there was "a question of abolishing services or paying more taxes for them," he believed the public would be willing to pay higher taxes.[43] However, rather than simply raising property taxes, Lark tried to pursue other options.

First, Lark looked into expanding the commercial tax base of the city. Lark knew that Cranston's residential property owners were bearing most of the city's financial load because Cranston lacked "the source of income that comes to most cities from industry."[44] This occurred due to the fact that Cranston was primarily zoned for residential living. Although Garden City hosted the first suburban shopping center in Rhode Island, Cranston had difficulty finding locations to zone for new businesses because the proximity of residential homes to potential business locations caused residential homeowners to object to almost any commercial development. Requests for spot zoning, in which a single parcel of land was rezoned differently than its surrounding area, inevitably led to an unappealing combination of angry neighbors, political controversy and costly litigation. Lark never resolved the problem of how to expand the commercial tax base in a predominately residential city. It remains an unsolved riddle for city officials to this day.

Second, Lark predictably sought more state aid, in particular for schools. But at the time, the state government was already providing about 20 percent of the city's income. Also, the state government was facing its own budget woes from the rapid growth in its own workforce, which led to the imposition of a new sales tax in 1947, even though state officials were being warned that Rhode Island had lost its tax advantage over other industrial states.[45] Out of options, Lark approved a series of property tax increases that took the tax rate from $2.30 per $100 to $2.80 per $100 in order to pay for a city budget that doubled, along with a city debt that also doubled. This startling increase in spending, taxes and debt occurred over a mere eight years.

As a community becomes more urbanized, residents enjoy various conveniences, but sometimes they must also endure crime. At this time, bookmaking began to appear in Cranston. Lark, who was born and raised in a small town in Iowa, wanted a "clean, moral city" and ordered a crackdown on illegal gambling after investigative newspaper reporting showed that "bookies were openly operating in Cranston."[46] Lark eventually grew frustrated with the Cranston police chief's efforts to stop gambling, so Lark brought charges against him for neglect of duty, specifically "failing to enforce gambling laws," and suspended him.[47] To Lark, it was "the most difficult thing" he had ever done in his life.[48] In his defense, Police Chief Nelson Bourret alleged that "political pressure" from Republican Party leaders was behind the move to oust him.[49] After three days of hearings and testimony from numerous witnesses, including two newspaper journalists, seven police officers, the police chief and the mayor, the city council found the police chief guilty of two charges of neglect of duty, and he was demoted to inspector.[50] Soon thereafter, he retired to collect a city pension, and the captain who had led the squad against gambling, Louis Fouchecourt, was made the new police chief.

The controversy surrounding gambling in Cranston and the ousting of the police chief a few months before an election were not the only problems Lark faced. The growth in Cranston's population after the Second World War had changed the city's political complexion. Before the Great Depression, stricter mortgage terms had made it more costly to build homes in Cranston, but with the change in home financing after the Second World War, building a home in Cranston was now within the economic reach of many more families. As a result, those who built homes in Cranston after the Second World War represented a "large influx of Democratic voters from Providence."[51] Unlike the mayoral races in 1946 and 1948, when he had received more than 55 percent of the vote, the mayoral race of 1950 was one of the closest in Cranston history, and Lark only won it by ninety-five votes, with 50.2 percent of the vote. Also, the Democrats won eight of the twenty seats on the city council for their best showing since the start of the First World War.

Believing that "no one man can or should be mayor too long," Lark decided against seeking reelection for mayor in 1952 and instead was elected to the more slow-paced state senate, where he represented Cranston for six years.[52] Although he had been suggested as a candidate for governor, Lark aspired to the tranquil life of a state judge, but to his great disappointment, it never came to pass.

During the 1950s, Cranston witnessed a new wave of school construction as its population rapidly grew. Mayor Lark "had pinpointed sites" for these new schools, and at the groundbreaking ceremonies for these new institutions, it became clear that he was "never happier."[53] In 1971, the year Lark died, Cranston was still confronting many of the same issues it had faced while Lark was its mayor. City services were expanding, property taxes were increasing, state aid was stagnant and fear of crime was on the rise. One other thing had not changed: schoolchildren were still attending the schools Lark had supported building in the 1950s, including the Garden City Elementary School, located less than a mile from his home, where he passed away quietly.

GEORGE R. BEANE

1953–1955

Although George R. Beane was an attorney, he was proudest of being a soldier. A West Point graduate, he had served in the Second World War, during which he was wounded, decorated with a Purple Heart and promoted to lieutenant colonel. He wanted not just to serve his country but also to lead his community. His political involvement began as a leader of the Young Men's Republican Club, and in 1939, he became the registrar of the State Motor Vehicles Department for two years under Governor Vanderbilt. When Lark bowed out of the mayor's race, Beane was quick to step in. Benefiting from having General Eisenhower as the Republican presidential nominee, Beane, the decorated officer, won the election with 55 percent of the vote in 1952.

Believing that with increased population there was a need for increased city services, Beane continued the fiscal policies of his predecessor. Cranston continued on its rapid rate of government spending, which led to more debt and higher property taxes. Plans were made to spend millions more to build additional schools and to provide sewer service to more parts of the city. As a result, the tax rate increased from $2.80 per $100 to $3.00 per $100, and the city began spending 20 percent of its $4.8 million budget just to pay debt service. But in the area of funding the pension system, Beane made an unfortunate departure from Mayor Lark.

In 1947, the city had begun to invest $10,000 per year into the pension system for firefighters and police officers, which, combined with the 1 percent payroll deduction from police officers and the 5 percent payroll deduction from firefighters, allowed the city to create reserves from which it was able to pay retirees without using revenues from the general fund. However, in lieu of granting firefighters a pay raise, the city council decided to reduce the payroll contribution for firefighters from 5 percent to only 1 percent.[54] As a result, by the end of the decade, the city was paying for pension benefits with money from its general fund rather than solely from the pension fund.[55] Thus, while reducing payroll deduction may have avoided granting a pay raise to firefighters in the short term, it ended up reducing the amount of the equity building in the pension fund and, in the long run, created a burden to taxpayers as the city veered back down the path leading to a large, unfunded pension fund. It took less than a decade from the establishment of a pension plan for firefighters for Cranston to completely discard the recommendations of its actuaries.

While his predecessor had increased the size of police department, the approach Beane followed proved more controversial. Although a study had recommended that the police department's patrol force be enlarged, Beane proposed that the police department be reorganized by increasing the number of superior officers. He made this proposal without consulting Police Chief Louis Fouchecourt. Opponents of Beane's plan ridiculed it by claiming that it was a scheme that would turn the police department into a "Mexican army" made up of more officers than privates. Because some of the officers slated to receive promotions under his plan had testified in defense of the former police chief, Nelson Bourret, who had been removed from office in 1950, some accused Beane of doing the bidding of party leaders who had backed the former police chief.[56] After it failed to garner enough support for passage on two prior occasions, a compromise was reached that increased the number of officers but also created a traffic division.[57] This was not the end of Beane's troubles.

Beane decided that the city needed a property tax revaluation to eliminate inequities in assessed property values that had built up over many years so as to better distribute the tax burden. However, as with any revaluation, some taxpayers' homes were assessed at a higher price, and as a result, these homeowners were required to pay more in taxes. Taxpayers received their tax bills resulting from the revaluation weeks before the election, which led to confusion and anger from some voters. The Democratic mayoral nominee, John Turnbull, seized the opportunity and claimed that Beane and the Republicans had broken their pledge not to raise property taxes in that year's budget. Accused of political interference at the police department, facing angry taxpayers who believed that he had broken his tax pledge and without Eisenhower on the ballot to help increase Republican turnout, Beane lost the 1954 mayoral election by approximately 3 percent.

Although defeated, Beane rallied his troops, and the Republicans went on the offensive. Since Republicans had controlled both the city council and the mayor's office for four decades, Cranston's city employees had all been appointed by a Republican. With a Democrat entering the mayor's office and Democrats getting closer to taking control of the city council, there was a fear that in the near future, city employees would lose their jobs to Democratic patronage seekers. A few weeks after the defeat in November 1954, the city council hastily adopted a civil service system covering many city employees, and a month later, just before leaving office, the city council appointed a personnel director, while Beane, with the consent of the city council, appointed members to a personnel appeals board.[58] Thus, a city employee could only be removed for cause.

Although the federal government had adopted a civil service system in response to the assassination of a United States president by a crazed job seeker, it seems Cranston adopted its civil service system in order to protect employees who had benefited from one party's patronage from the patronage seekers of another political party. After protecting the jobs of hundreds of city employees, the Republicans decided to hire a few more city employees. At this same lame duck session, Beane and the city council enacted a dramatic reduction in the work hours for firefighters and then quickly appointed fourteen new firefighters. The Democrats objected that the cost of these new firefighters would put the city's recently adopted budget into the red, but it was to no avail.[59] In politics, a deficit is not an obstacle when patronage is possible.

After leaving office, Beane faded away from the public eye, but the civil service protections he started during his brief term still endure. Beane's life came to an end at the age of eighty-three in 1984, the same year that Cranston sent out tax bills after completing its first citywide property revaluation since 1954, the one that had ended Beane's political ambitions.

Transformation

John Turnbull

1955–1957

For the first half of Cranston's city history, most of Cranston's mayors all shared at least two traits. They were Republican in politics, and they were older in age. There were only two exceptions: the first mayor, Sullivan, a young Democrat who briefly turned Cranston's local politics upside down, and the tenth mayor, John Turnbull. Like many others with young families, Turnbull moved to Cranston after the Second World War. When he ran for mayor as a Democrat in 1954, Turnbull was not expected to win. When he won with 51.5 percent of the vote by carrying the Democratic-leaning Third and Fifth Wards by large margins, it came as a surprise. As a result, Turnbull became the first Democrat-elected mayor in Cranston in over four decades, and at age thirty-two, the youngest man ever elected mayor of Cranston.

After shocking Cranston's Republicans on election day, Turnbull would surprise them once again on inauguration night. Under Cranston's charter established in 1910, the mayor had limited administrative and appointive powers. However, under the city council's rules, the mayor had the authority to appoint city council members to various committees. Fearing how a Democratic mayor would exercise this power, the Republican city council majority planned on adopting new rules that would strip Turnbull of this authority and restrict the powers of the Democratic minority. In his inaugural speech, Turnbull denounced the Republicans' proposed rule changes. After his speech, he took the gavel and recognized a Democratic city councilman who proposed a Democratic version of rules for the city council. Banging his gavel over the objections and shouts of the enraged Republicans, Turnbull called for a voice vote and ruled that the Democratic version of rules had been adopted and then ruled that the Democrats' motion to adjourn had also passed by a voice vote. The Democrats left the chambers. After a brief delay, the Republican majority resumed the city council meeting, at which they passed their version of rules and called Turnbull a disgrace.[60] Eventually, a compromise on the rules was reached, which allowed Turnbull to make appointments to committees with some restrictions while also increasing the influence of the Democratic minority over the legislative process. Turnbull had yet more surprises for his Republican adversaries.

Turnbull quarreled with city council Republicans on engineering contracts for new sewer construction work. At a city council meeting, Turnbull recognized a Democratic city councilman who produced a letter from the city's bond counsel stating that the city could not issue sewer bonds for work in some of its neighborhoods because they were outside the district covered in the enabling legislation. Republicans loudly complained that Turnbull was playing politics and delaying necessary sewer construction, but Turnbull believed that the city council needed "to learn its lesson" the "hard way."[61] Turnbull's tactics scored political points, but they also delayed sewer service for various neighborhoods.

Not surprisingly, Turnbull wrangled with the city council Republicans over city finances as well. Republicans condemned Turnbull for using the city's contingency fund to pay $900 in bills involving a softball tournament by the American Legion at Cranston Stadium. In turn, Turnbull criticized the Republicans' deficit spending budgets, but in the end, Turnbull did not veto their budgets, which increased spending by 30 percent over two years and raised the property tax rate again.

Turnbull had a variety of other squabbles with the Republican-controlled city council.[62] However, his battle with the Republicans paled by comparison with the war he had with Cranston Democratic Party chairman Michael Sepe, the brother of the once prominent state representative Walter Sepe. Party bosses like their candidates strong enough to win on election day but weak enough to be directed once they are elected. Turnbull's relationship with Sepe became strained when Turnbull would not defer to him. After other internal party issues arose, Turnbull tried to oust Sepe but was unsuccessful. Later, at the Cranston Democratic Party's endorsement meeting, Turnbull was endorsed, but he then rejected the endorsement, and a fight involving a pocketknife nearly ensued between a Sepe backer and Turnbull's secretary.[63]

In this political theater, the campaign of 1956 was conducted. The Republicans nominated the elderly city council president Earl A. Colvin, who promised to restore "dignity" to the mayor's office. Republicans attacked Turnbull for making a "mockery" of the mayor's office, being dictatorial and seeking "publicity."[64] In the end, Turnbull was defeated by 2 percent when he failed to win the Democratic Third and Fifth Wards by the same

Transformation

percentages he had won them two years earlier. Thus, in attempting to grasp control of the Democratic Party, he had lost his hold on the mayor's office.

Subsequently, Turnbull acknowledged that not much "positive" legislation had passed while he was mayor, but he still planned to run again.[65] Instead, Turnbull quietly left Cranston and moved to Florida in 1958. He would reemerge on the public stage in 1962, when he was indicted on two counts of federal tax fraud for money he had received while he was mayor. Although he claimed the charges were "politically inspired," Turnbull pleaded guilty to tax fraud for 1956 and paid a fine, while the other count was dismissed.[66] Later, in tax court, Turnbull disputed these taxes, and the judge agreed with Turnbull about his taxes for 1955 but ruled against him on his taxes for 1956 because he had already pleaded guilty to tax fraud for that year.[67] Later, he would return to Rhode Island and run for Congress as an Independent in 1992. Turnbull knew he would not win the race but simply wanted "to be heard"; he finished in fourth place behind another Independent who had also experienced tax troubles.[68] Today, he is an elderly man residing in California, but for some, Turnbull will always be the young man pounding a gavel on inauguration night to ensure that the minority would be heard.

EARL A. COLVIN

1957–1961

When Cranston became a city in 1910, it was called a "city of farms" because it was predominately agricultural, but only one mayor, Earl A. Colvin, was ever a farmer.[69] Colvin was a dairy farmer whose family had lived in Cranston for generations. Before becoming mayor, he served on the city council for a decade, like his father before him. After years of tax increases and watching the debt grow, the elderly Colvin campaigned for mayor on "holding the line on taxes" and reducing the city's debt. With the

Democrats under Turnbull battling one another, Colvin won with 51 percent of the vote in 1956.

In the dozen years since 1945, the city's property tax rate had increased by nearly one-third, and the city's debt had more than tripled. Colvin believed that "if you continue to borrow, the ultimate and final result is bankruptcy." Thus, Colvin's primary focus was to avoid further tax increases or increasing the city's debt by trying to control spending. To accomplish this, Colvin knew he could "not increase services" or "increase salaries" because it would lead to "increasing taxes." This proved a difficult task to achieve. Colvin found that the "hardest part of being mayor" was "the constant pressure from one particular group or another" to spend money. Although he resisted it, he admitted "it is not easy to say no" Although Colvin knew that the "easy course would be to spend, to yield to every pressure, and to borrow money promiscuously and leave the debts to be paid for by our children and our grandchildren," he was not about to leave a legacy of debt to future generations.[70]

A dozen years after the Second World War, the city's debt tripled largely because of new school construction. Believing that a large debt was dangerous, Mayor Colvin had Cranston High School West built in phases.

Transformation

Most of the city's debt had been accumulated for new school construction since the end of the Second World War. In the most recent six years, the construction of nearly ten schools had been started in the city. Colvin believed that a large debt jeopardized the health of a city, and he wanted to economize school construction. Also, Colvin knew that new schools required more teachers and an "endless chain of increases" leading to tax increases.[71] As a result, Colvin declared that the city's school construction had been "too ambitious" and decided to slow down the pace.[72] He had the new junior-senior high school in western Cranston built in phases because he felt that building it all at one time was too extravagant. As a result, the city's debt level shrank by nearly 10 percent during Colvin's four years as mayor.

As for taxes, after an initial tax rate increase to $34 per $1,000 in 1957, necessitated by the serious financial problems caused by the city's spending habits in prior years, the budgets adopted during the Colvin administration never required a tax increase for the remainder of his time as mayor. His labors resulted in a $100,000 surplus for the city in 1958. The voters respected his frugality but only rewarded his efforts by reelecting him by a narrow margin, with 51 percent of the vote, in the election of 1958. In that election, Colvin carried the First, Second and Fourth Wards, and the Republicans held a twelve-to-eight majority on the city council, reflecting Cranston's evenly divided electorate in this decade.[73]

Colvin's second term was more turbulent, with many battles with different foes. In his effort to hold the line on taxes and control spending, Colvin focused his attention on the school department, which spent the largest part of the budget. When the school committee granted a raise to teachers, Colvin and the city council, on a party line vote, refused to fund it and reduced the request from the school committee. Democrats attacked the Republicans for having a surplus by calling it "overtaxing" and said that the surplus was large enough to pay the increase in teachers' salaries. Colvin defended the need for a surplus by stating that lenders looked favorably on Cranston's having a reserve and compared the city's reserve to a "rainy day" fund, which should only be used "for any emergencies."[74] This type of debate would arise whenever the city had a large reserve.

When teachers complained, Colvin, the mild-mannered country farmer, called the president of the teachers' association, a forerunner to the teachers' labor union, a "stooge for a certain few radical leaders in our school system," and said that "as soon as they win the battle for one raise," they start "seeking the next and the next raise."[75] Prior to this confrontation, Colvin had warned about "certain selfish labor leaders" and "special interest groups" that seek much more than a "few paltry dollars."[76] He also emphasized that Cranston teachers were well paid and received a pension for working fewer than 190 days a year and wondered "how many of the taxpayers" earned the same as teachers.[77] By comparing public employee pay to private sector pay, Colvin was adopting a tactic that would be used by future elected officials in trying to win public opinion against giving in to the demands of public employees for higher pay and benefits.

The battle with the schools put the first dent into the popularity of Colvin and the Cranston Republicans, but Colvin and his party's hostility to the home rule charter movement would wreck it. Cranston was governed by a charter that was enacted in 1910 by the Rhode Island General Assembly in which the mayor had very limited administrative powers and administrative oversight of city government rested primarily with the city council through its subcommittees. Some believed this was highly inefficient, and thus there was a need to change the charter in order to increase the powers of the mayor. There were two approaches to change the charter. One was through a legislative process by which the city council proposed a new charter and the Rhode Island General Assembly adopted it. The second, as allowed by an amendment to the state constitution in 1951, was through a petition signed by 15 percent of the voters to have a special election to determine whether a charter commission should be established, and then the voters would elect charter commission members to draft a new charter for voter approval.

While leaders of both parties in Cranston disagreed on much, they agreed that a new charter should be adopted through a legislative process, which required approval of the Republican-controlled Cranston City Council and the Democrat-controlled Rhode Island General Assembly. They both feared the kind of charter that would emerge from a charter commission elected by the voters. Sometimes mutual self-interest and fear create the strongest of political bonds. A petition drive to create a home rule charter commission occurred from 1954 through 1956 but ran out of momentum. Later, in 1959, it was renewed, and the petition signatures were filed with the Cranston Board of Canvassers. In an attempt, to thwart their efforts, Michael Sepe, a Democratic state representative and chairman of the Cranston Democratic Party, helped pass a bill that would have invalidated any signatures collected more than one year prior to their submission to a board of canvassers. When Republican governor Christopher Del Sesto vetoed the bill, the Republican-controlled Cranston Board of Canvassers adopted rules to invalidate any petition signatures collected more than a year prior to their submission. The proponents of the home rule charter movement appealed to the Rhode Island Supreme Court. In the meantime, Republicans on the city council adopted a new charter that strengthened the powers of the mayor. The Rhode Island General Assembly passed it, but Governor Del Sesto vetoed it. In response, Colvin led a walkout of Cranston Republicans at a party fundraiser when Governor Del Sesto was about to speak.[78] Shortly thereafter, the Rhode Island Supreme Court reversed the decision of the Cranston Board of Canvassers, and an election on creating a charter commission was set.[79]

In addition to these battles with the School Department and government reformers, Colvin was immersed in accusations related to machine politics. Colvin's administrative assistant, Malcolm Daniels, was also chairman of the Cranston Republican Party. Unlike the party bosses of old, who worked quietly behind the scenes, the young, abrasive Daniels played a key role in city government. The grandfatherly Colvin was accused of being a mere puppet of Daniels and the mayor in name only.[80] In his dual role, Daniels combined the influence of a party boss with the powers of a public official and made himself an easy target for Colvin's political opponents. Daniels's hard ball tactics drove many Republicans out of office, from city department heads to councilmen to state legislators.[81] As a result, an independent movement emerged called the Good Government Party, consisting of many dissident Republicans led by Frank J. Calcagni. Calcagni had been the leader of the Citizens' League, an association in favor of a home rule charter, and he had been appointed by Colvin to the chairmanship of the Cranston Industrial Commission, which was a board established to attract business to Cranston. As if that were not enough, Cranston's largest employer, Leesona, formerly Universal Winding Company, decided to move south to Warwick after complaining of rising taxes and lack of suitable space in Cranston for its business to expand.[82] The departure of Leesona was a blow to Colvin, who had viewed industrial growth as "the only salvation for the City of Cranston" financially.[83]

In the midst of this turmoil, a troubled Colvin went on vacation to Vermont to contemplate the situation. Upon his return, he announced that he would "bail out the school committee" and grant the teachers a retroactive pay raise; out of fairness, he would also give a raise to city employees. Colvin justified this decision on the basis that the state had just given Cranston about $400,000 in additional aid, and with a surplus of over $800,000, or approximately 10 percent of the city's budget, the raises could be paid with no tax increase.[84] His opponents saw it differently. Francis R. Dailey, the Democratic mayoral nominee and minority leader on the city council, said that Colvin's about-face was an attempt to salvage his administration. He

Cranston was once called a "city of farms." The Oak Lawn Grange, built in 1914, is a reminder of that bucolic bygone age.

claimed that since the surplus had been that large for a year, Colvin was trying to win over the "voting strength of the city workers."[85]

Throughout the 1960 campaign, Dailey attacked Colvin's surplus as over taxation, attacked Colvin's administration as a "Moscow-like machine rule" and championed higher pay for government employees.[86] One of the most colorful campaigns in Cranston history ended with Dailey defeating Colvin, 44.6 percent to 39.5 percent, with 15.9 percent going to Calcagni. More importantly, the Democrats took control of the city council, for the first time in four decades, by a lopsided margin of fifteen to five. Colvin could not survive the split in his own party and the massive Democratic turnout in favor of Kennedy, the Democratic presidential nominee. It was the "end of an era." Colvin, the Yankee agrarian who had been a charter member of the Oak Lawn Grange, had succumbed to Dailey, the Irish worker who had organized the first labor union at the Cranston Print Works. As Cranston's population grew, so had its government, and as a result, the city had transformed. Cranston was no longer the small nineteenth-century town of mostly farms in which Colvin was born, the town that existed before the advent of the electrified streetcar system.[87] Cranston was now a changed city of over sixty-five thousand people.

Knowing that in politics you "can not please everyone" and instead you must simply "do what is right," Colvin was stoic in defeat.[88] Believing he had done what was right, Colvin died shortly thereafter on his farm in 1964 at the age of seventy-one. Colvin's opponents admitted that, as mayor, he was honest and frugal, and so he remained to his last day, true to the values he had learned all those years ago on his father's farm when Cranston was still just a small town.

Challenges

1961–1984

Francis R. Dailey

1961–1963

For a half century, nearly all of Cranston's mayors had either legal backgrounds or had managed enterprises in manufacturing, entertainment or agriculture. This was not the case with Francis R. Dailey, who, as a textile worker at the Cranston Print Works, had organized and become the leader of the first labor union at the company.[1] After becoming a labor leader, he naturally became a political leader. Dailey served on the Cranston City Council for eighteen years, representing the heavily Democratic Fifth Ward, and eventually became the city council's minority leader. In 1960, Dailey became the Democratic mayoral nominee. With local Republicans divided and Kennedy winning Cranston, only the second time the Democratic presidential nominee had carried Cranston since the demise of the Sprague financial empire, Dailey won the mayor's race by 5 percent in a three-way contest, and the Democrats took over the city council, fifteen to five.[2] For the first time since 1913, the Democrats controlled both the mayor's office and the city council.

Being more than four decades out of power, the Democrats were eager for patronage. Many city department heads and employees who served at the pleasure of the city council were replaced with Democrats. But no matter how large government becomes, it is never large enough to satisfy all those who seek its patronage. Democrats on the city council split into factions over the distribution of patronage.[3] When the patronage and power available seemed insufficient, Dailey and the Democrats focused their attention on the zoning board of review. The Republican appointees on the zoning board could not easily be dismissed, so the Democrats decided to abolish the board. They justified it by claiming the board lacked representation from members of both parties. They then reconstituted the board with mayoral appointees who were members of both parties. Republican city councilmen claimed it was a "farce" since they did not know any of these "Republican" appointees. A Democratic councilman responded that now the shoe was on the other foot.[4]

After seizing the reins of government, Dailey decided to expand it by creating new agencies. Under Dailey, Cranston's Redevelopment Agency was established to rehabilitate the blighted neighborhoods that were arising in the sections of Cranston that bordered Providence. Also, Dailey created the Cranston Housing Authority, which, with federal funding, would build low-rent apartments for low-income households, originally just low-income seniors. After President Lyndon Johnson declared a "war on poverty" in 1964, Cranston began participating in federal antipoverty programs. A half century before, Cranston had started as a city of farms; it then became a suburb that served as the bedroom of Providence, and now it was becoming an urban city with low-income housing, troubled by blight and combating poverty.

After distributing government jobs and creating new government agencies, Dailey decided to dramatically increase government spending. In two short years, the city budget increased by 15 percent. The primary reason for this increase was salary increases for government employees. As a labor leader in the private sector, Dailey had sought higher pay and better benefits for employees from the profits of shareholders. As a public official, he carried this mentality over and advocated for higher pay and better benefits for government employees from the taxes of the public.

Challenges

The federally funded Cranston Housing Authority built low-rent apartments for low-income households. Hall Manor, Cranston's first public senior housing complex, was built in 1965.

In 1961, a "relatively unknown bill" passed the Rhode Island General Assembly that allowed firefighters to organize unions and required municipalities to collectively bargain with them.[5] Cranston firefighters were quick to take advantage of this new law. Dailey showed that management did not need to have an adversarial relationship with labor.[6] In September 1962, the Cranston firefighters' union reached the first collective bargaining agreement for public employees in Rhode Island with Dailey, the man who had organized the first union at the Cranston Print Works. It was a precedent-setting arrangement rich with symbolism. Firefighters received significant pay increases that were reflected in the budget adopted just before the election of 1962 by Dailey and the Democratic city council. Firefighters were granted a 12 percent raise, making them the second-highest-paid firefighters in the state.[7] Firefighters were not the only city employees to get pay raises. In the budget, police officers got a 12 percent raise, making them the third-highest-paid police officers in the state, and city employees received a 6 percent salary increase.[8]

In addition, Dailey and the Democrats granted Cranston's city employees, who were not firefighters or police officers, a pension plan by entering the pension system managed by the State of Rhode Island for municipal employees.[9] A Democratic councilmen called it one of the "finest humane acts" he had seen, but this compassion did not arise from purely altruistic motives.[10] Republican councilmen pointed out that a city councilman would be eligible to receive a pension for his years of part-time service on the city council under this plan. Apparently, the labors of part-time elected officials merited full-time employee benefits. To balance the budget, Dailey did not raise taxes "in an election year" but instead tapped much of the reserve that his predecessor, Colvin, had saved.[11] To one mayor, a reserve is for emergencies; to another, it could be used to pay routine operating expenses. Republicans warned of future tax increases because of these pay raises, while Democrats denounced the Republicans for caring more about the surplus than giving "working people" a "living wage."[12]

In the 1962 mayoral election, Dailey emphasized his creation of new governmental agencies while not raising taxes. Dailey's slogan was that "one good term deserves another," but he did not get another. In another close mayoral election, Dailey lost by 2 percent of the vote, and the Democrats lost control of the city council. His Republican opponent, James DiPrete Jr., was able to unite the divided Republicans and reverse the prior Republican Party position on a home rule charter by campaigning in support of it.

But defeat did not end Dailey's interest in public service or his interest in helping city employees. In a lame duck session in January 1963, Dailey and the Democrat-controlled city council adopted an ordinance that required pensions for firefighters and police officers to be based on their pay at the moment of retirement.[13] A few years later, in 1968, this ordinance allowed J. Howard Gibbs to become police chief for "the ridiculous reign of five minutes" and to retire on a pension based on a police chief's salary.[14]

Dailey later became the executive director at Cranston's Housing Authority, the agency he created, which was managed by a board he had appointed. He served as its executive director until 1965 and saw the completion of Cranston's first public senior housing complex, Hall Manor. He later retired under the city employee pension plan that had been adopted while he was mayor and received a pension based on his eighteen years of part-time service as a councilman and his two years as a mayor.[15] Dailey had worked his whole life to increase the pay and benefits of working people. In his golden years, Dailey, a workingman himself, would reap the benefits of what he spent a lifetime promoting.[16] He died in 1997, a year before the Democrats would regain the mayor's office for the first time since he was mayor.

Challenges

JAMES DIPRETE JR.

1963–1971

Like many Cranston mayors before him, James DiPrete Jr. was an attorney, but he was the city's first "strong" mayor under the new home rule charter. DiPrete began as a young assistant city solicitor under Mayor Colvin and first garnered public notice in 1960, when he defended, at the Rhode Island Supreme Court, the rules adopted by the Cranston Board of Canvassers that had invalidated certain signatures on petitions supporting a home rule charter election. After his court defeat and the electoral defeat of Mayor Colvin in 1960, he would reemerge as the Republican candidate for mayor in 1962, but this time as advocate for the adoption of a home rule charter. DiPrete's dexterity had an explanation.

In 1960, the advocates for a home rule charter had won the legal right to have a special election for the creation of a home rule charter commission. A majority voted in favor of creating a charter commission, but because of a split among home rule charter advocates, the majority elected to the charter commission had been endorsed by the Republicans and had never supported the home rule charter movement. DiPrete, who had once been "dead set against" a home rule charter and "bent over backwards to kill" it, now jumped "on the home rule bandwagon."[17] By changing his position on the home rule charter, he was able to win back the support of government reformers.

However, this was not the only break DiPrete made with the positions of the Colvin administration. DiPrete also parted ways with the controversial Malcolm Daniels, Colvin's former assistant and Cranston Republican Party chairman, who was blamed for the Republican defeat in 1960. As a result, in 1962, DiPrete won the Republican mayoral primary by defeating two other candidates: the candidate supported by Daniels and Calcagni, who had been an Independent candidate for mayor in 1960. Not only did Daniels's mayoral candidate lose, but also Daniels himself lost his seat in the Cranston Republican Party in that same primary and lost the party chairmanship. For the general election, DiPrete and the Republicans made the home rule charter the "principal issue in the campaign with Republicans strongly favoring it and the Democrats maintaining mostly silence."[18] Bolstered by the wide margin by which the proposed home rule charter was adopted, the thirty-five-year-old DiPrete won the mayoral election with 51 percent of the vote, and the Republicans regained a slim majority on the city council. DiPrete owed his political life to the home rule charter he had once opposed.

The popularity of the new home rule charter was due to the efforts of its proponents, who viewed the charter as a "cure all of Cranston's ills."[19] Periodically, government reformers emerge who believe that the ills of government can be cured by changing its structure or its processes rather than by limiting its powers. For the more powers a government has, the more likely it is to be corrupted. The new charter created a "strong mayor" who could efficiently administer all city departments and established a merit-based civil service system, a nonpartisan school committee and open government requirements. The new charter also changed the distribution of power. It "gave the mayor broad hiring and contract powers."[20] The mayor now appointed nearly all department heads. He controlled who was awarded city contracts, since a majority on the Board of Contract and Purchase constituted himself and his appointees, and this same majority could waive the requirement for competitive bidding for any contract. The authority to hire and the ability to award contracts were concentrated, directly and indirectly, in the office of the mayor. These new far-reaching mayoral powers could be used as patronage in order to garner campaign donations and campaign volunteers, the building blocks of a political machine. At the time, some recognized that the creation of this "strong mayor" could prove to be "very dangerous."[21] The more that power is concentrated, the more likely it will be abused.

DiPrete, an adroit politician, shifted away from the Colvin administration not only on the home rule charter and Daniels but also on controlling school spending and reducing the city's debt. While Colvin had reduced the city's debt, DiPrete embarked on an ambitious capital improvement program that included building a new police station, an addition to the fire headquarters and a wave of school construction, including more elementary schools, such as an elementary school in Glen Hills, and a new junior high school to reflect the continued growth in Cranston's population.[22] He also continued the accelerated expansion of sewer services, which was paid in part with

Challenges

federal funds. By the end of the decade, he was beginning the expansion of water service into western Cranston. These capital improvements increased the city's debt and caused the city's debt service requirements to double in eight years.

Where Colvin had battled with the school committee and teachers over school spending, the politically astute DiPrete wanted to "alleviate the tension" between the city and the School Department. As a result, DiPrete became an "advocate of fiscal independence for schools," including giving the school committee taxing authority. In an attempt to avoid the "annual school wrangle" between the School Department and the city over school funding, DiPrete would not attempt "to substitute his judgment" for that of the school committee in matters of school funding.[23] Coupled with a 20 percent increase in student enrollment, Cranston's school budget more than doubled in eight years.

In order to pay for this massive increase in spending, DiPrete planned for the further development of Cranston. He unveiled and won adoption of the first major revision of Cranston's zoning map since 1924. It allowed Cranston to keep its "rural character" in the far western section of Cranston, but it also allowed for industrial development in western Cranston along the proposed path of Route 295. Like a pioneering frontiersman, DiPrete

Glen Hills Elementary School was built in 1964 as part of a new wave of school construction reflecting the continued growth in Cranston's population.

believed that Cranston's future lay in the west. However, some criticized DiPrete's plan because it did not prevent proliferation of residential plats, "which enrich their developers and burden the city" with the need for more city services when, instead, Cranston was in dire need of more industrial development.[24]

Cranston's industrial development was lagging, and as a result, DiPrete needed to increase property taxes to pay for services to Cranston's growing residential community. Although DiPrete was a "strong mayor" under the new charter, the independent city council still had taxing authority. In the first two years, the city council was controlled by DiPrete's own party, but it was miffed at the transfer of much of its former powers to the new mayor under the new charter. DiPrete and this city council would even clash over how meetings should be adjourned. When DiPrete proposed a tax increase from $34 to $39 per $1,000, the city council rejected it and instead used more of the city's reserve, lowered school funding and estimated higher tax revenues—the usual budget maneuvers used to avoid a tax increase without actually cutting municipal spending. Accordingly, the School Department ran deficits, teenagers protested at Cranston City Hall over cuts in school sports and schools opened two weeks late—the usual response of the school committee when the city cuts school funding. It was not until 1965 that the city council finally agreed to raise property taxes to $39 as DiPrete had originally proposed back in 1963.

While DiPrete was seeking peace with the school committee and waging battles with the city council, he was entangled in a war within the police department. Cranston's police department had been the scene of many melodramas since the first mayoral administration. This was due, in part, to the political process by which city employees were hired and promoted prior to the adoption of the home rule charter. Previously, the mayor had generally made appointments or promotions at the police department with the consent of the city council based on the "recommendations made by the ward committees of the political party in power."[25] The new charter created a merit-based personnel system with civil service protections that required examinations for promotions—a development many police officers welcomed. However, for some police officers, promotions based on examination and civil service protections were not sufficient. Luckily for them, in 1963, the same year the new charter went into effect, the Rhode Island General Assembly passed legislation allowing police officers to form unions.

In the wake of the new state law, some of Cranston's police officers began to take steps toward forming a union.[26] At the same time, DiPrete began firing certain police officers for such infractions as being intoxicated on the job or sleeping in a patrol car.[27] However, DiPrete's most controversial disciplinary action was when he suspended seven officers for insubordination because, as board members of Cranston's Fraternal Order of Police, they had voted to boycott written promotion exams on the basis that patrolmen were "unable to find material to use in preparing" for the exam. A majority of the police officers who sought promotions ignored the boycott and took the exams.[28] After word of the boycott found its way to the press, DiPrete suspended the seven police officers who had voted for the boycott. However, DiPrete's suspensions were later reversed when the Rhode Island Supreme Court found a lack of evidence that these seven officers had notified the media of their vote to boycott the exams.[29]

DiPrete called for an investigation into the unrest and absence of discipline at the police department. Eventually, outside consultants were retained to study and reorganize the police department. In 1964, their report found that the police department suffered from "political interference" and "favoritism."[30] This favoritism led to factionalism. Police officers split into union and non-union camps, with union backers fearing favoritism and wanting duties and promotions meted out by seniority and union resisters wanting duties and promotions based on one's ability and alleging that "those who resisted joining the union were pushed around by those who did."[31] To some, a seniority system protects incompetence, while to others, a merit-based system promotes cronyism. Eventually, in 1964, in its first contract, the Cranston police union's "major gain" was obtaining "stricter seniority rights."[32] Through the years, public employee unions would strive to have more and more aspects of the management of public employees governed by strict adherence to seniority.

Despite his advocacy for higher property taxes and his troubles in the police department, DiPrete won reelection in 1964 with a solid 55 percent of the vote, and then, in 1966, he won a four-year term with a smashing 64 percent of the vote while carrying all six wards and helping the Republicans win an eight-to-one majority on the city council. Cranston Republicans had not enjoyed such a victory in a quarter century. With his "broad hiring and contract powers" as mayor, DiPrete had created an effective political organization built on "patronage" and "fundraising."

In the meantime, Democrats were in disarray. In 1966, Michael Sepe, the longtime Cranston Democratic Party chairman and an influential state representative, lost his state representative seat in a Democratic primary after generating unfavorable attention for trying to expand horse betting.

Claiming that Sepe had a "totally unacceptable image" and blaming him for the Republican control of Cranston when a majority of its voters were Democratic, his fellow Democrats voted him out as party chairman.[33] With Daniels's defeat in 1962 and Sepe's defeat in 1966, the power of Cranston's old-fashioned party bosses had ended, and in their place stood DiPrete, who had "pioneered the modern style of political fundraising," which was not dependent "on party efforts."[34] Making the most of his landslide victory, DiPrete decided to run in a special election for an open congressional seat in 1967 but lost by a few hundred votes. Instead of contending with national issues like the Vietnam War, DiPrete would have to grapple with a force that would prove more powerful than the powers of a "strong mayor"; namely, public employee unions. His battle with public employee unions would turn into a quagmire that would consume the rest of his time in office.

A few weeks after his congressional election defeat, negotiations broke down between DiPrete and the police and firefighters' unions. The police and firefighters' unions wanted higher pay, fewer hours, better benefits, advantages for seniority and a requirement that all members of the fire and police departments belong to the union. DiPrete could agree to some of their demands and offered an 8 percent raise, but he resisted the request of firefighters to reduce their work hours because they spent "part of their workweek sleeping," and he would not budge on requiring all police officers and firefighters to be union members, thereby creating a union shop.[35] Having a union shop was particularly important to the police union because one patrolman, tired of being "harassed like other non-union members," went to court to protect his "right to work without forced union affiliation."[36]

As a result, the police and firefighters' unions began picketing city hall, as well as the police and fire stations. When employees from the public works department crossed the picket line under DiPrete's orders to work on the parking lot at the new police station, they became "the victims of threats," and their wives were "taunted by savage phone calls" that "threatened the safety of their husbands if they continued to cross the lines."[37] When DiPrete stood firm, Frank Montanaro, leader of the firefighters' union, referred to the dispute as "combat," and picketing spread to all public construction sites in Cranston, thereby disrupting school and sewer construction, even though school officials warned that delays could jeopardize the accreditation of certain schools.[38] One newspaper editor stated that the "picketing of schools under construction" was a "way to make the residents come to their knees" and that the "unions want the Mayor to crawl on his belly and bend to their will."[39] Republicans warned that "if the city gives in this time to this pressure"

Challenges

Mayor Jim DiPrete confronted numerous challenges involving the Cranston Police Department. As Cranston's financial foundation was beginning to crack, Cranston's newly built police station began to sink into the ground due to faulty construction in 1971.

then "there will be no way to stop these men in the future." Apparently, labor leaders responded by saying DiPrete was "bent on breaking up the unions" and calling him a "monomaniac" and a "dictator."[40] The city was split between those who believed that DiPrete wanted to bust the unions and those who believed that the unions wanted to bust the city.

After a judge put a halt to their picketing at schools by declaring it was designed "to coerce, compel, force and bludgeon" city officials, the Rhode Island Labor Relations Board found DiPrete guilty of unfair labor practices and ordered him back to the negotiating table.[41] Eventually, this decision was reversed by a judge, and DiPrete asserted that the labor board was "unfair to employers" and warned how the labor board "could be used as a weapon to bludgeon employers into submission."[42] In the meantime, police officers who were willing to accept an 8 percent raise and saw the picketing as a "power play of a few misguided union officials" formed a rival union.[43] At first, it appeared that these police officers were gathering strength, but then the Rhode Island Labor Relations Board decided in favor of the existing union by determining that the election of the new union was "untimely."[44]

Cranston's police and fire labor unions then turned to other labor unions across the state for support and finally to the state legislature for a solution. A state association of firefighters censured DiPrete, and its leader pledged to "mount a lobbying campaign for compulsory binding arbitration that will shake the foundations of the State Capitol."[45] In 1968, legions of firefighters and police officers descended on the state capitol in support of binding arbitration for firefighters' and police unions. In response, the General Assembly passed the desired legislation over the near-unanimous objections of municipal officials, who said that binding arbitration would take away the ability to set tax rates from elected officials and average citizens at town financial meetings.[46] A compliant Republican governor, John Chafee, signed the bills into law with no formal explanation while his spokesman suggested that binding arbitration should be "given a try."[47] Just as Rhode Island's textile strikes of 1922 and 1934 had altered the course of this state's history, so would the enactment of binding arbitration after a year long labor dispute in Cranston.

While binding arbitration was being considered at the state capitol, DiPrete had decided to come to terms with his labor foes, so alone among the state's mayors, he supported binding arbitration. He soon reached an agreement with the firefighters' union in which "the union won much of its major demands, shorter working hours and more pay," including a 14 percent reduction in their work hours and a 13 percent raise in their pay. However, DiPrete was able to hold firm on giving firefighters "the option of not joining the union."[48] In the week leading up to the 1968 election, he reached three-year agreements with the firefighters' and police unions, which made them "the highest paid in the state" and gave them contracts that were "among the best" that could be found "anywhere in the country."[49] Montanaro, the firefighters' leader, was so pleased that he said "he would send copies of the contract to unions in other cities" in the hopes that cities would "follow Cranston's example."[50]

As for the police contract, it came after the first binding arbitration decision was made, under the newly enacted law, a decision in which the union won on "its three major demands in the dispute."[51] When the agreement was signed, the police labor leader stated that, just as "President Johnson had ended the bombing in Vietnam," so had "DiPrete ended the war in Cranston"—an interesting analogy.[52] DiPrete's temporary labor peace came at a price. The property tax rate, which had been increased to $43.80 in

Challenges

1967, was increased to $49.40 in 1969. The budgets for the police and fire departments had doubled in eight years.

DiPrete's truce with labor did not benefit him politically on election day 1968. Due to high Democratic turnout for the presidential election, Democrats gained a seven-to-two majority on the city council in a "surprising show of strength."[53] DiPrete's truce also proved to be unilateral on his part. With a huge Democratic majority on the city council, the firefighters' and police unions saw an opportunity to increase their pension benefits, something they had not been able to achieve through collective bargaining. In 1969, on a party line vote, the Democrats on the city council adopted an ordinance that allowed police officers and firefighters to retire with a full pension after only twenty years of service rather than twenty-five. This was done in addition to recent pension enhancements for police and firefighters and despite clear warning signs that the financial stability of the pension fund was in trouble.

During the 1960s, pension benefits were liberalized for Cranston's police officers and firefighters. For instance, in 1965, DiPrete and the city council approved of ordinances that gave police and firefighter retirees, those already retired and those who would retire in the future, pension increases that equaled the pay increases given to active members of the police and fire departments.[54] These "escalator" ordinances provided pension increases that exceeded a typical cost-of-living adjustment and proved to be "a major cause of the soaring unfunded liability" of the police and fire pension fund.[55] Also, these same ordinances granted an unusual birthday gift to both police officers and firefighters when they turned the age of fifty-five: an increase in their pensions by 5 percent.[56] As a result, in three years, pension costs doubled, and in 1966, an actuarial study showed that the police and firefighters' pension fund already had an unfunded liability of $3 million.

As part of the ordinance that lowered the service requirement to receive a pension from twenty-five years to twenty, Democrats increased the pension payroll deduction for police and firefighters from 1 percent to 3 percent of their salaries. However, this amount was still lower than the 6 percent contribution paid by other city employees, who received less generous pensions. Furthermore, it was clear that this increase in the pension contribution would "fall far short" of covering the additional cost for this pension enhancement.[57] Either realizing, at long last, the financial perils facing the pension fund or simply angered that the unions had circumvented him and had not acted in good faith during collective bargaining, an infuriated DiPrete vetoed the ordinance. He noted that no other police or fire department in Rhode Island had as generous a pension plan as Cranston for its public safety employees. He emphatically declared, "I cannot emphasize strongly enough that the City of Cranston cannot possibly afford the lavish proposals contained in this ordinance."[58] Although the city council overrode his veto, DiPrete refused to enforce the ordinance and declared it illegal. The Rhode Island Supreme Court, while acknowledging "that the union was the motivating force behind the introduction of the 1969 ordinance," still found the ordinance valid, even though the enactment of the ordinance seemed inconsistent with "the delicate nuances attendant to true collective bargaining."[59] The cost of this retirement enhancement would prove to be "more lavish than anyone imagined," and eventually "some Democrats privately conceded that the ordinance was a mistake."[60]

At the start of the 1960s, Cranston's police and fire pension fund had assets totaling approximately $124,000, but by the end of the decade, there was barely $12,000 left in the pension fund. At the beginning of his term, DiPrete had warned the city council that it was "wrong to charge today's expenses to tomorrow's taxpayers."[61] Regrettably, it took until the end of his term for DiPrete to realize that all of the pension benefits he had given as mayor would have a tremendous cost to the taxpayers of tomorrow.

A few months later, in 1969, DiPrete decided to leave public service. As a father of four children, he needed to make money so he could send them to college. He did not seek reelection in 1970 and instead joined a prominent law firm. Although he never served in elected office again, DiPrete remained active in politics. In 1980, he became the chairman of Ronald Reagan's presidential campaign in Rhode Island.[62] After Reagan won the presidency, DiPrete was rewarded with a job as regional administrator of the Department of Housing and Urban Development and became embroiled in a controversy involving the "nation's only known federally subsidized housing for the elderly built on a flood plain."

Beginning in the late 1970s, low-income housing for the elderly had become a lucrative field due to large federal subsidies for apartment owners. The exemption to build on a flood plain was urged by the regional office of HUD and "reeked of favoritism and influence peddling."[63] A partner in the firm that built this controversial housing was a cousin of DiPrete, as well as his business partner in another building's ownership. While admitting that the events surrounding the exemption were "so coincidental, it would almost strain somebody's credibility" and acknowledging that he "probably should

Challenges

have" disclosed his relationship with his cousin's firm on his financial reports to HUD, DiPrete vehemently denied any wrongdoing, and he was never charged with any.[64]

At the time of his death in 1993, DiPrete was hailed as "a founding father of Cranston's Republican machine" and "credited with forging a Republican powerhouse" that "controlled the City for three decades."[65] However, the machine that he built, under the "strong mayor" charter, did not survive him for very long. In 1994, the powers of the "strong mayor" were diminished through the adoption of amendments to the home rule charter. In 1998, the machine he built collapsed under the combined weight of high taxes, an unfunded pension debt and widely publicized scandals.

JAMES L. TAFT JR.

1971–1979

To become the mayor of Cranston requires political skills, but few Cranston mayors loved politics as much as James L. Taft Jr. Taft's father had been a "dominating factor" in Cranston politics for years.[66] Reared in the world of politics, Taft began holding public office while still in law school, when he was appointed by Mayor Beane to be on a city charter study commission. He became a city councilman, a state senator, chairman of the Cranston Republican Party and then minority leader in the Rhode Island Senate in 1969, all before he turned forty years old. After his close ally and friend Mayor James DiPrete Jr. decided to return to private life, Taft decided to make politics his full-time profession by seeking the office of mayor. In the 1970 mayoral election, Taft ran on the accomplishments of DiPrete and his own governmental experience while advocating for more federal and state aid for Cranston, specifically for hosting the state prison. The young Taft won the election with 51 percent of the vote, defeating the Democratic nominee, who was the youngest city council president in Cranston history.

From the outset, as mayor, Taft saw the "disintegrating condition of the fiscal structure" for cities and how property taxes alone could not support the level of services that cities provided. To Taft, the problem of high property taxes would be "finally solved only" with "other sources of revenue" coming from the federal and state government. But this was not an ideal time to seek more state aid, since in 1971, Rhode Island adopted an income tax to address its own budget problems. In the meantime, Taft saw that Cranston needed to expand its tax base, in particular by developing western Cranston, although he promised that this new westward expansion would not result in "profiteering" or a "land grab."[67]

Cranston's financial foundation was clearly on shaky ground, but it would be the foundation of the newly built Cranston police station that first cracked. In 1971, just a few years after it was built, Cranston's new police station began to sink into the ground due to its faulty construction.[68] While the police station was sinking, property taxes were rising. Knowing that Cranston was in some financial difficulty, and that it was better politically to have a tax increase at the beginning of his administration, Taft decided to raise property taxes in 1971. Blaming the prior Democrat-controlled city council for spending the surplus through overestimating revenues and underestimating expenses, Taft proposed raising the property tax rate from $49.50 to $56.00 per $1,000.00. The Democratic majority on the city council agreed to raise taxes but blamed it on the three-year contracts the former Republican mayor had signed with the police and fire unions. After this initial significant tax increase in his first year, Taft was able to avoid a property tax increase for the next year and actually reduced it to $55.00 per $1,000.00.

In 1973, Taft was able to obtain millions of dollars from the federal government in the form of revenue sharing and, soon thereafter, more federal funding through the Comprehensive Employment and Training Act (CETA). CETA was enacted to help "municipalities get through a recession" while giving unemployed residents training at "temporary" jobs.[69] Instead, Taft used CETA funds to pay the salaries of an expanding police department and for the addition of firefighters for the new Sockanosset fire station near Garden City.[70] Staffing at the police department grew by 32 percent, and staffing at the fire department grew by 23 percent during the 1970s, while during the same time period, Cranston's population actually declined.[71] By 1978, 40 percent of city employees were funded through CETA. In addition,

Challenges

Under Mayor Taft, federal CETA funds were used to expand government payrolls and pay for additional firefighters at the new Sockanosset fire station near Garden City.

Taft was able to obtain Community Development block grants, and with other federal money, he began providing new city services and programs, such as transportation for the elderly.[72] Instead of a "life-line" for cities, it became "a heaven-sent opportunity" for politicians to obtain patronage and "stall inevitable increases in local tax rates."[73]

By 1974, spending had continued to grow, fueled in part by "runaway inflation" from higher energy prices. Taft's efforts to gain state aid for providing services to state facilities in Cranston had proven unsuccessful. Balancing a budget requires either more revenues, usually through higher taxes, or lower expenses, usually in the form of reduced personnel costs or program cuts. Higher taxes anger taxpayers. Personnel cuts anger government employees. Cuts in services anger the constituents who use the services. All are unappealing options to a politician in an election year. But a skillful politician knows there are always other options, one being creative accounting. Taft presented a budget in 1974 with no tax increase by changing the city's accounting practice in order to recognize "all revenues paid to the city in the fiscal year in which it is paid," which meant that taxes prepaid in

June for the upcoming fiscal year starting in July would not go toward the next fiscal year starting in July but instead would be used to pay expenses for the fiscal year ending in June. In other words, "spend today what you think you'll collect tomorrow." It was a form of deficit spending, since it used revenues for the next fiscal year to pay the expenses in the current fiscal year. Democratic city council president Anthony DeLuca denounced Taft's proposal regarding prepaid taxes as a "scheme to deceive the citizens of Cranston" that would "prove disastrous in the future." However, the intricacies of accounting are less appealing to voters than a candidate calling himself the "Working Mayor," who campaigns on three years without a tax increase while providing more services to seniors and increasing police and fire protection. Taft won reelection with 70 percent of the vote, the highest-winning percentage for a mayor since the boom years of the 1920s, and he brought a Republican majority to the city council as well.[74]

Taft was on top and looking to move higher. He began contemplating a run for governor, but before he could run for statewide office, he had to address local budgetary problems. With the city facing "the twin economic terrors of recession and inflation," which created a "vise-like grip producing a squeeze of rapidly rising costs and decreasing revenues," Taft called for more federal and state aid.[75] When more aid was not forthcoming, Taft proposed a property tax increase of $3.70 per $1,000.00 but the tax increase only provided an increase in the school budget of about 1 percent, about $200,000.00, instead of the $2.5 million originally requested by the school committee. Eventually, negotiations between the school committee and the Cranston teachers' union broke down when teachers wanted a raise greater than 5 percent, and a teachers' strike delayed the school opening for a few weeks.[76]

Realizing that providing insufficient school funding had only added to his problems, Taft looked to obtain more revenue from expanding the tax base. In his first term, Taft's efforts had caused the General Assembly to set aside state-owned land for the creation of the Howard Industrial Park, but businesses were slow to move there. In his second term, Taft looked to expand the tax base through development in western Cranston. Partly due to Taft, water service was already reaching western Cranston by the mid-1970s. After the water started to flow, the developers began a land rush. In the fall of 1975, the Planning Commission unveiled a new zoning plan, the first since the mid-1960s, which included zoning for apartment complexes in western Cranston. This led to furious opposition from residents of western Cranston because they wanted to maintain western Cranston's rural character. A group of these residents organized and specifically opposed any apartment complexes at Wilbur and Natick Avenues. A series of hearings at the city council filled with "tension and anger" occurred. Although Taft offered various compromises, which reduced the number of potential apartments, city officials stubbornly refused "to even consider a site for apartments other than in the Wilbur and Natick avenues area."[77]

Eventually, the leader of the group opposed to the rezoning accused city council president Edward DiPrete of having a conflict of interest, since DiPrete's mother owned land that would be zoned for apartments. DiPrete labeled the accusation of a conflict as "ridiculous" and said that people can question his decisions but not his integrity.[78] With accusations of unethical conduct being made, and overwhelming opposition to rezoning spreading throughout the city, Taft held a dramatic press conference at the end of 1975 in which he switched his position and opposed the proposed rezoning, effectively killing the proposal.

In 1976, Taft surprised no one when he announced a run for governor, but he surprised many when he proposed a property tax rate increase of $4.80, which raised the rate to $63.50 per $1,000.00. To some, it showed the "financial strain" facing Cranston, while to his Democratic critics, it showed that Cranston was "on the brink of disaster" from having been sent "along the path of deficit spending."[79] In his gubernatorial campaign, Taft called the Democratic statewide political organization a "machine" and promised to "pull the plug on the machine," while back in Cranston, his Democratic critics alleged that Taft ran a Cranston political machine. On election night, Taft carried Cranston by 13 percent but lost the governor's race by 10 percent, and the Republicans lost control of the city council. The rising political star had fallen back down to earth.

Returning to Cranston City Hall after a hard-fought campaign, Taft engaged in a series of very personal battles. First, he sought and obtained the dismissal of Police Chief George Coffey on the grounds of insubordination and misconduct.[80] To some, the whole dispute appeared to be a "personality conflict."[81] Next, Taft and the Democrat-controlled city council bickered in what some called the "best show in town."[82] Charges and countercharges were made over the smallest issues, and the city council president, Anthony DeLuca, nearly resigned at one point.[83] When Taft proposed a budget in 1977 that raised taxes, the Democrats reduced the tax increase to $4 by increasing revenue estimates and reducing expenses. Taft angrily vetoed the budget, saying it would lead to $1 million deficit, and noted that the entire spending increase in the budget went to the School Department because two of his chief critics on the city council were Cranston schoolteachers. His veto was overridden.

Eventually, the budget deficit for that year reached nearly $2 million, exacerbated by the cost associated with the Blizzard of 1978. When the deficit became apparent, Democrats called on Taft to use his authority under the charter to cut spending, but he refused to cut senior services or community programs. The "demand for city services, many of them nonessential," had "outstripped the taxpayers' ability to pay," and as a result, a "deficit occurred." One newspaper editor speculated that Taft would not cut his "favorite programs" because it would cost him a "considerable number of votes."[84] After a ruling by the state auditor, Taft finally agreed to discontinue the use of prepaid taxes, and in 1978, the property rate was hiked from $67.00 to $76.95 per $1,000.00, an increase of $9.95, in an effort to gradually reduce the city's deficit over five years. In 1978, a private audit showed that the city had accumulated a deficit of approximately $5.3 million, of which $3.3 million was due to the use of Taft's prepaid taxes and about $2 million was due to the deficit caused by the budget passed by the Democrats in 1977. This deficit constituted over 10 percent of the city's operating budget.

Democrats blamed Taft for the use of prepaid taxes and his failure to cut spending in the budget passed in 1977, while Taft blamed the city council Democrats for passing a flawed budget in 1977 and noted that they had adopted his prior budgets, which used prepaid taxes. While the politicians blamed one another, a newspaper editor could only express his astonishment at "the lack of foresight demonstrated" by Cranston public officials "during this decade."[85]

The cumulative deficit of $5.3 million was not the only major financial problem for the city. It was dwarfed by the unfunded police and fire pension fund. In 1973, the Democrat-controlled city council formed a special commission to study the police and fire pension fund.[86] The consultant hired by the commission recommended that the city stop paying for pensions out of the general fund, under the pay-as-you-go approach, and instead institute a self-supporting system by fully funding the pension system with a required annual actuarial amount. Having difficulty finding money to balance the budget and paying current expenses, Taft rejected the consultant's plan. In 1977, the police union brought legal action to require the city to fully fund the pension system, but a judge ruled that the city was not legally required "to keep a sound pension fund." As a result, the unfunded pension liability grew to $32 million by this time, and one newspaper editor talked about "the legacy" for "future generations of Cranston residents" being a "bankrupt city."[87]

Despite these troubles, Taft ran for reelection in 1978 to face city council president Anthony DeLuca, his most persistent critic, in what promised to be a memorable campaign. However, the best-made political plans are subject to the hand of fate, and in August 1978, Taft's brother-in-law and partner in the family law practice suddenly died. Taft decided not to continue his run for reelection and instead went back to run the law firm to support his family and that of his deceased brother-in-law. In his place, Republicans nominated Councilman Edward DiPrete, who went on to win the office of mayor.

Although Taft left the mayor's office to be a full-time lawyer, he stayed involved in politics and mixed his two interests in ways that proved both highly profitable and highly controversial. He became Governor DiPrete's political and business partner. Taft served "at the helm" of Governor Edward DiPrete's "political organization." His law firm served as the "heart of the DiPrete machine."[88] Taft, well known "for his knowledge of local zoning laws," became a business partner of Governor DiPrete in a company that obtained a zoning variance, over the objections of neighbors, to allow for the construction of a luxury apartment building, and then this company purchased and sold this parcel of land on the same day for a profit of nearly $2 million.[89] The controversy became known as the "Cranston Land Deal." Also, under Governor DiPrete, Taft's law firm became one of the top three law firms providing legal services to state government. This led to a fine from the Ethics Commission, which was upheld by the Rhode Island Supreme Court; it was an ethical violation for Governor DiPrete to give government legal business to Taft's law firm since he and Taft were business partners.[90]

Those days are just faded memories now. Taft is retired from law and politics, but his law firm, the one his father established just before Taft was born, still remains in Cranston. Taft was called a "politician's politician," but sometimes politicians cannot see beyond the next election. At the height of the bickering between the city council and Taft in 1977, Taft wrote an angry veto message about the budget in which he lectured the city council Democrats that their decisions "will plague this community far beyond your political career." The same could have been told to Taft.[91]

EDWARD D. DiPRETE

1979–1985

Few men rose as high, or fell as far, as Edward D. DiPrete. DiPrete started as the owner of F.A. DiPrete Realty, a local Realty company that had been established by his father. DiPrete's involvement in politics occurred by chance when he decided to run for the school committee after coming home one night to find his boys reading the sports page for homework. He went on to become chairman of the Cranston School Committee and then president of the Cranston City Council. It was not by design that DiPrete became a candidate for mayor in 1978 but the result of the unexpected death of Mayor Taft's brother-in-law and law partner. With the help of former mayor James DiPrete, his cousin, and Taft's organization, DiPrete waged a short mayoral campaign that focused on fixing the city's finances and ending the bickering at city hall. DiPrete edged out city council president Anthony DeLuca by 43.6 percent to 42.0 percent in a three-way race.

With the city facing a $5.3 million deficit, DiPrete did not exaggerate in his inaugural address that "these are not the best of times"; he noted the "extreme pressures between the cost of government and our ability to pay" for it.[92] After four straight years of tax increases, including a 15 percent increase in Taft's final year, many expected that DiPrete would seek a tax increase in his first year in order to pay off the deficit and to keep up with double-digit inflation. DiPrete amazed all by not seeking a tax increase in his first budget and won applause from Democrats. In fact, in his six years as mayor, DiPrete sought only one property tax rate increase in 1981, of 7 percent, and was able to erase the $5.3 million deficit by 1982.[93]

DiPrete was able to accomplish this by focusing on increasing revenues other than through a general property tax rate increase. First, DiPrete tried to obtain higher revenues from a small number of properties in Cranston,

Challenges

primarily rural farmland in western Cranston and some apartments. DiPrete had decided that the tax-assessed value of these properties was too low since the land was zoned for industrial use and had access to water and sewer services. For one farmer, this meant an increase in property taxes from $2,000 to $72,000 per year. Farmers complained and noted that throughout the nation, farmland was taxed at how it was used rather than how it was zoned. Farmers believed that DiPrete was resorting to unfair taxation to drive them off their land in order to further economic development. Their allegations were denied, but one city official admitted that "the bottom line" for Cranston was that "the City is pro-industrial development" because "the City needs the revenues in order to hold down the taxes."[94] It was another round in the battle between those who want to preserve rural beauty and those who want more development in order to gain more tax revenues.

In the end, the courts agreed with the farmers and other property owners that DiPrete's selective reevaluation was illegal.[95] But this legal victory

Before a tax reevaluation under Mayor Ed DiPrete helped cause farmers to sell their land to developers, cattle could be seen grazing on the pastures of western Cranston. *Courtesy of Cranston Historical Society*.

proved only a temporary reprieve for the farmers and a temporary obstacle to the spread of development. When a state-mandated revaluation began in 1983, some farmers decided to sell because the higher taxes would make it "economically unprofitable to farm."[96] Farmers became developers and turned in their plowshares for real estate licenses. As a result, Cranston began to lead the state in issuing single-family residential building permits. However, this residential housing boom gave only a temporary boost to tax revenues since the revenues would soon be offset by the demand for more government services.

Second, DiPrete tried to generate more revenue through the expansion of the tax base by enticing more businesses to locate in Cranston. DiPrete helped establish the Western Cranston Industrial Park. Although this area had been zoned for industrial use since 1966, it was not until the early 1980s that DiPrete had sewer lines extended to the area. However, while new businesses were appearing in the west, the eastern part of Cranston was losing many of its oldest and largest businesses. In just a handful of years in the early 1980s, Narragansett Brewery, which had been established nearly a century earlier, in 1890, closed due to the high costs associated with energy and workers' compensation; United Wire closed due to a lengthy labor strike; and Ciba-Geigy closed due to a lack of space for expansion and after battles with neighborhood residents over environmental concerns.[97] Cranston was no longer a "manufacturing city" as it had once been called during the First World War. Instead, Cranston's largest employers were now governmental entities like the state, the School Department and the city— employers that consume rather than generate tax revenues.[98]

Third, DiPrete took advantage of the unique situation in which inflation had caused very high short-term interest rates. DiPrete adopted an "aggressive investment policy" in which the city invested its funds to take advantage of these high rates. To increase the amount of funds he could invest, DiPrete delayed capital projects. For example, in his first year as mayor, capital spending was decreased by 85 percent. DiPrete would borrow before the city needed it and invest the borrowed money. By having the city borrow money at lower long-term interest rates, the city was able to generate large amounts of revenue by investing funds in high-interest, short-term certificates of deposit. For instance, the City of Cranston generated $257,000 in investment income in 1978, but in 1982, it was $2 million. The city's investment policy was "a major reason" for the elimination of the deficit.[99]

Spending grew during the DiPrete administration, but at a slower rate than in the past. In the area of school spending, DiPrete noted that

Challenges

"while there has been a huge drop off in enrolled students, the numbers of people teaching them has remained substantially the same."[100] However, declining enrollment was occurring during a time of rapidly rising prices and increasing demands by teachers' unions that believed that "a quality education is the best salaries and benefits combined with the smallest possible class size."[101] DiPrete attempted to exert more control over school finances and reduce spending increases by calculating school funding on a per-pupil cost. As a result, personnel was laid off, schools were closed, sports programs were temporarily ended, school deficits arose and school committee members were investigated for charging the school system "for everything from political donations to entertainment at conventions."[102]

As for city spending, DiPrete's efforts did not lead to layoffs. Instead, he retained city employees, despite the termination of federal funding of the CETA program under President Ronald Reagan. Most noticeably, DiPrete retained many senior service jobs started under Taft. While some Democrats alleged that, "under the guise of helping" seniors, DiPrete "created patronage jobs," DiPrete made no apologies for the money spent on senior programs or on the senior center he established.[103]

In a few city departments, spending increased dramatically under DiPrete. Spending on the fire department more than doubled in six years, while the police budget grew by approximately 80 percent. However, this increase was partly beyond DiPrete's control. Under the Taft administration, public employees unions had continued their forward march. In 1972, city employees began receiving family health insurance, and because of binding arbitration, union leaders won the requirement that employees either had to join the union or pay an amount equal to union dues to the union if they wanted to retain a city job.[104] In 1975, the firefighters' union, through binding arbitration—and soon thereafter, other city unions—through negotiation began receiving longevity pay bonuses, which give employees additional pay raises the longer they stayed working in government.[105] In 1976, seniority became a factor in promotions because the Rhode Island Supreme Court ruled that a binding arbitration decision affecting the promotions of firefighters could trump regulations made pursuant to a city charter.[106]

In the 1980s, while federal public employee unions and Rhode Island's private sector unions encountered severe defeats, Rhode Island's public employee unions would continue to achieve great victories. In 1980, a "neutral arbitrator," who was the spouse of a high-ranking pro-labor Democrat,[107] made a binding arbitration decision that required Cranston to provide "Blue Cross to retiring firemen for the rest of their lives," even though firemen could retire in their early forties after twenty years of work. DiPrete blasted the decision as removing "any incentive for a man to remain with the fire department for more than the minimum twenty years," which, he estimated, would increase pension costs by 23 percent. In the same decision, this neutral arbitrator established a minimum manning requirement for firefighters, which required DiPrete to hire more firefighters and increased their overtime. DiPrete denounced this aspect of the decision as an invasion of management prerogative and noted that "Cranston already has substantially more firefighters" based on its population "than other cities."[108] As a result of minimum manning and the opening of a new fire station on Scituate Avenue in western Cranston, the fire department's staffing increased by more than 10 percent, while Cranston's population grew by less than 5 percent during the 1980s. A year later, in 1981, in another binding arbitration decision, this time made by "neutral arbitrator" who was a Democratic Providence city councilman, holiday pay was "included in determining a retiree's pension."[109] DiPrete denounced the "one-sided" decision and called for stripping arbitrators of their binding authority.

In 1983, legislation developed by the League of Cities and Towns to remove pensions, other retirement benefits and staffing issues from binding arbitration died in the General Assembly, although it was supported by

The fire station located in western Cranston on Scituate Avenue was built in the same decade in which Mayor Ed DiPrete battled the firefighters union in binding arbitration.

many municipal leaders.[110] DiPrete blamed its defeat on Frank Montanaro, the leader of the Cranston firefighters' union, who was also the leader of the statewide association. What the firefighters won through binding arbitration, police officers in Cranston gained by contractual agreement out of a sense of fairness and a feeling of futility in contesting the issue in binding arbitration.[111] Three decades later, the unfunded liability of retiree healthcare for police and firefighters would reach over $50 million.

After erasing the $5.3 million deficit in 1982, primarily through a short-term increase in revenue, DiPrete turned to the long-ignored, multimillion-dollar, underfunded police and fire pension fund. The pension fund liability had been made worse by the recent arbitrators' decisions and agreements to include longevity pay in the pensions. With pension benefits increasing, DiPrete decided to increase funding to pay for these benefits. First, DiPrete tried to get employees to contribute more toward their pensions. In 1982, DiPrete was able to convince police officers to increase their contribution to the pension fund from 3 percent to 7 percent of their pay gradually over four years and to have newly hired police officers contribute 8 percent. Second, DiPrete had taxpayers put money into the pension above what was immediately needed to be paid out to retirees. As a result, in 1983, DiPrete set aside an additional $200,000, and then in 1984, an additional $600,000 was added to the pension fund. DiPrete's efforts were a small step forward, but more than small steps would be needed to address an unfunded liability that "was already out of control."[112]

Being able to wipe out the $5.3 million deficit with only one property tax rate increase while maintaining popular city services made DiPrete a very popular mayor. With the help of his popularity and his fundraising prowess, Republicans regained control of the city council in 1980, and in 1982, DiPrete won reelection with 83 percent of the vote, a record unmatched to this day. His popularity was so elevated that one political analyst called it "god-like."[113] As one would expect, the confines of Cranston seemed too small to forever house the political future of DiPrete. Although he initially refused to seek the governorship in 1984, once the Democratic incumbent, Joseph Garrahy, decided to retire, DiPrete entered the race with an announcement that was compared to a "Hollywood production."[114] His star continued to rise. He went on to win the governorship in a landslide following a bitter Democratic primary.

His star reflected the brightness of a strong national economy, and his successes continued. One supporter called his first two years as governor "the two best years in recent history" for Rhode Island.[115] In 1986, he would win reelection with 65 percent of the vote, the highest percentage for a Republican gubernatorial candidate in a century. Then the luster began to fade. In the middle of 1988, there was the "disclosure of questionable contract awards and other dealings," such as the Cranston Land Deal.[116] DiPrete won reelection in 1988 by only a few thousand votes. His lucky star seemed to vanish as an economic recession came and, with it, massive tax increases and unbalanced budgets. In 1990, he lost the governorship in a landslide.

But this was not all that would befall DiPrete. After leaving office, grand jury investigations revealed an aspect of his administration that few suspected and many were appalled to learn. Apparently, since his days as Cranston mayor, DiPrete had headed "a pay-to-play system" in which government contracts and favors were awarded based on "hefty campaign contributions and outright bribes." Lurid tales were told under oath. There was evidence that a sewer contractor "had padded his construction bills in Cranston and paid kickbacks to Cranston city officials," including paving DiPrete's driveway for free. There was testimony that DiPrete personally selected contractors, received a free trip from a city vendor and took money from a developer seeking a zoning change. Memorably, there was the story of DiPrete rummaging through a restaurant's trash to retrieve a bribe he had mistakenly tossed out. After many legal twists, DiPrete pleaded guilty to eighteen counts of bribery, racketeering and extortion, served nearly a year in prison and lost his pension. However, DiPrete still maintained his innocence and said that others were guilty of corruption; he claimed that he had accepted the plea agreement so that his son, who was also charged in the case, would not risk going to prison. Leery of the public spotlight that had once shined so warmly on him, DiPrete now spends most of his time looking after his ailing wife and basking in the love of his family.[117]

In his first mayoral inaugural address, DiPrete had said that "the course of our lives can suddenly and profoundly be changed by an event, which is least expected," and so it was for DiPrete. However, DiPrete's public career was guided not only by stars of fortune but also by motivations within him. It is human nature to focus on the failures of a man rather than on his successes. It is easy to forgot that at one time DiPrete was a mayor who had a "record of achievement" and a man who "would be remembered as one of Rhode Island's better, perhaps best, governors" before he was called "a figure whose name is forever blackened in the annals of Rhode Island" after he left prison.[118] For DiPrete, the good and the bad all happened on such a grand scale that it makes it difficult to reconcile all the aspects of his public life into one coherent perspective. For some, the story of Edward DiPrete was a classic tragedy; to others, it was an epic of corruption. But most likely, it will remain a riddle for historians to resolve someday.

CRISIS

1985–PRESENT

MICHAEL A. TRAFICANTE

1985–1999

No man served longer as mayor of Cranston than Michael A. Traficante, but originally Traficante had no ambitions to be mayor. Instead, he aspired to be the principal of the school from which he graduated. He was a Cranston math teacher, a popular coach and, later, an assistant principal at Cranston High School East. Then his life took a different direction. Although he was a political neophyte, at the urging of Mayor Taft, Traficante ran and was elected to the city council in 1978. Two years later, when the Republicans gained control of the city council, he became president, and when Mayor Edward DiPrete was elected governor, Traficante became acting mayor in 1985. A few months later, he won a special election by nearly a two-to-one margin to fill out the remainder of DiPrete's term based on his "immense popularity" and his promise to continue providing a high level of city services.[1]

At the time Traficante became mayor, Rhode Island was at the beginning of an economic upswing fueled by a real estate boom.[2] The real estate boom helped increase the property tax base of Cranston, while economic growth increased state revenues, filtering down to cities and towns in the form of increased state aid. As a result, Traficante had the ability to provide more services, better pay for public employees and increased education spending while minimizing the need for increasing property taxes. However, Traficante's first two years were not all smooth sailing. While state government was becoming more generous with aid to cities and towns, the federal government, facing large budget deficits, eliminated federal revenue sharing with the cities, which led to a cut for Cranston of approximately $1.4 million annually. Traficante labeled these cuts as an "urban massacre" and stressed how Rhode Island already had one of the highest property tax burdens in the nation.[3]

Despite these problems at the federal level, in his first budget, Traficante increased spending by nearly 10 percent with no tax increase. However, the school funding increased by only about 5 percent, with Traficante stating, "I don't believe massive infusions of money alone will create a better public school system."[4] When the school committee complained and suggested its usual cuts related to closing neighborhood schools, eliminating sports programs or reducing busing service, an annoyed Traficante dismissed it as just the school committee's annual griping about budget cuts. At this time, the school committee was arguing not only with Traficante over budget items but also amongst itself over chairmanship of the committee. All of this led Traficante to suggest changing the city charter to make school committee members appointed rather than elected officials or to give them their own taxing authority.

After this initial quarrel, Traficante took a more accommodating approach with the school committee that would continue throughout his administration. In his next budget, Traficante proposed to give the School Department the exact amount it had requested, a first that avoided the annual tug of war between city hall and its School Department. Traficante was able to accomplish this without increasing the property tax rate even after the elimination of federal revenue sharing by using one-time revenue sources, such as $600,000 from the city's surplus—its rainy day fund—and from proceeds of the sale of surplus city properties. City council Democrats, specifically Peter T. Pastore Jr., criticized the use of sale proceeds to balance the budget and instead argued that sale proceeds should be used to pay down debt. However, the Democrats were ignored, and the budget was passed on a party line vote. At about this time, Traficante began his reelection campaign by trumpeting how he had given the schools all that they had asked for in his recent budget and had not raised taxes for two years. In the mayoral election of 1986, Democrats nominated Anthony DeLuca, the former city council president who had narrowly lost the mayoral race in 1978. Deluca criticized Traficante for his "credit card" approach to finances and told voters that there would be a tax increase next year because of Traficante's use of one-time revenue sources to balance the budget.[5] Voters ignored these warnings, and Traficante won reelection to a full four-year term by nearly a two-to-one margin.

Although the Democrats proved unsuccessful at winning the mayoral election, they proved to be excellent forecasters of municipal finances. In 1987, Traficante raised the property tax rate by 10 percent from $28.20 to $31.25 per $1,000.00, which exceeded the cap on property tax increases under a state law passed in 1985. However, Traficante found an exception in the law allowing for a tax increase above the 5.5 percent cap by suggesting that the city's inability to sell additional properties to generate one-time revenues or the ability to use more money from the city's surplus constituted a loss of revenue under the law. Also, Traficante considered a recent change in federal tax law designed to prevent cities from engaging in arbitrage by borrowing money in order to reinvest it at higher rate, as Cranston had done under Mayor Edward DiPrete, another revenue loss. While arguing the city had experienced revenue losses, Traficante proposed increasing spending by over 10 percent. This budget demonstrated a key aspect of Traficante's approach to taxes and spending throughout much of his time as mayor. If Traficante had to "choose between raising taxes or scaling back services," he would opt "for a tax increase."[6]

Traficante took pride in the level of city services provided by Cranston and justified the high taxes on that basis. Although Traficante was a Republican, he freely admitted that he was "very service-oriented" and had "more Democratic leanings than Republican leanings."[7] As a result, during his fourteen years as mayor, Traficante oversaw a significant increase in the level of city services directed at seniors and youth, both educational and recreational. Traficante built numerous tot parks and a youth center. He increased the school budget from $32.0 million to $78.3 million in fourteen years, meaning that, on average, the school budget increased about 10 percent every year under Traficante, thereby ensuring that Cranston's spending per pupil exceeded many other communities. He built a multimillion-dollar

Under Mayor Traficante, Cranston saw a significant increase in the level of city services for youths, including the building of the Cranston Youth Center.

senior center, which provided comprehensive transportation, as well as hot meals, dancing, beauty contests and Olympic-style contests. To Traficante, this senior center became the "showcase for our City."[8] All of this came at a cost that could be postponed but not avoided. However, in 1988, Traficante was able to propose a budget that increased spending but avoided a tax increase. In the fall, satisfied voters returned a Republican majority to the city council. At the same time, a credit rating agency dropped the city's bond rating because of its "financially troubled sewer fund."[9] Despite recent large increases in sewer fees, there was a deficit in the sewer fund of approximately $6 to $8 million caused by the city using its general funds to pay for sewer expenses. It was an early warning signal.

As some Democrats suspected, another non-election year brought another property tax increase when, in 1989, Traficante proposed to increase the property tax rate by $2.25, to $33.50 per $1,000.00, a 7 percent increase. Traficante made it clear that "reducing municipal services was never an option," and once again, the Republican majority on the city council acquiesced, although this time, because one Republican had broken ranks with Traficante, the tax rate adopted by the city council was one cent lower than what Traficante had proposed. While some of Traficante's critics were calling him "Tax Hike Mike," others applauded him in his spending increases for the School Department since they believed that his predecessor had shortchanged the schools.[10]

Shortly thereafter, the economy began to slow, but government spending continued to grow. As a result, the state government needed to make cuts in its budget, and rather than trimming the areas where spending was growing the fastest or where the amounts spent were the largest, the state government decided to cut where the opposition would be the weakest: aid to cities and towns. Governor DiPrete proposed a 25 percent reduction in state revenue sharing to cities and towns. Traficante called it a "crisis"—the first of many he would face—and proposed that the unions give up contractual pay raises for six months. The unions, in some instances unanimously, rejected the proposal, with the leader of the firefighters' union stating, "It's not the fault of the fire union" that Cranston is getting a cut in state aid.[11] As a result, Traficante was forced to do what he had always previously avoided during an election year; namely, to raise the property tax rate. In 1990, he had increased the property tax rate by seventy-five cents to $34.25 per $1,000.00, avoiding an even higher increase by using almost half of the city's surplus, equal to approximately $1 million, to balance the budget. However, the voters did not blame Traficante for these problems, and he was reelected by nearly a two-to-one margin.

Although a new Democratic governor, Bruce Sundlun, took office in 1991, the same approach of balancing the state budget in part by cutting aid to cities and towns continued, and now the cuts included state aid for education. After seeing a potential cut of approximately $2.5 million in his approximately $100-million-dollar budget, Traficante sounded the alarm of another budget crisis. In addition to state aid cuts, a souring economy had caused new home construction in Cranston to plummet and the city's tax base to cease expanding. To help alleviate his fiscal problems, Traficante again approached the unions to forgo pay raises, and this time, the police and firefighters' unions, the city hall employees and eventually the laborers did agree to forgo a pay raise for one year, but with a 5.6 percent raise in the next year of their two-year contracts. In the end, Traficante proposed a property tax rate of $37.35 per $1,000.00, or an increase of $3.10 (about 10 percent). When opponents of the tax increase organized and called for layoffs, city employees so packed the auditorium where the city council would meet that the "anti-tax increase people could not get in and be heard," while "the cheering section" of the pro-tax increase contingent in the hall was "led by a block of uniformed police officers."[12] In the end, the Republican majority made a few cuts to Traficante's budget, such as eliminating health insurance coverage for members of the city council, but it approved a tax rate increase of $2.92 while voting down many of the benefit cuts proposed by the Democrats. This tax rate increase was subsequently reduced to $2.59 when the state budget adopted by the General Assembly restored a portion of the state aid that Governor Sundlun had originally proposed to cut.

The next year, in 1992, the city finances were still troubled, but Traficante did not propose a tax increase and instead decided to once again use a one-time revenue source to balance the budget—more sale proceeds from surplus properties—and based his budget on the assumption that the unions would again not take a salary increase. He also proposed cuts to various social service agencies and a one-year moratorium on city contributions to various community organizations, including Cranston's one-hundred-year-old volunteer firefighter companies. The volunteer firefighters protested and noted that they were asking for $116,000 a year, less than 1 percent of the total cost of Cranston's unionized full-time fire department. Eventually, the city council passed a budget that contained no tax increase but allocated only $25,000 to the volunteer firefighters. After the budget was passed, unions agreed to delay pay raises and accept deferrals. While this budget was being considered, something more troubling than the city's troubled finances was disclosed.

A crafty California politician once said that "money is the mother's milk of politics," while a Christian saint once wrote that the "the love of money is the root of evil." Sometimes in politics, events occur that show the veracity of both statements. In 1992, a public corruption probe by the Rhode Island attorney general was made into the Traficante administration in an offshoot of the corruption probe of Governor DiPrete. First, the public works director was arrested for bribery and kickbacks, then the parks and recreation director was arrested for bribery and kickbacks and then the attorney general disclosed that Traficante and his director of administration, who had resigned just before news of the indictments broke, were targets of a criminal investigation involving a scheme to get cash campaign contributions from city vendors.[13] Democrats, led by Councilman Michael Sepe, the son of a once-influential Cranston Democratic Party chairman, called for an independent forensic audit of the city's finances, but city council Republicans blocked it, and the debate became so heated that Sepe and Traficante had to be separated.[14]

Since 1984, Traficante had raised nearly $1.7 million in campaign donations, spending money not only on his own race but also to benefit

Republicans running for city council. The amounts he raised were so large that subsequent Cranston mayors have not matched these numbers. Through his campaign war chest, Traficante was able "to maintain unchallenged political control" of Cranston for eight years with the bankrolling of city council races.[15] Now, it would prove to be a source of the "most humiliating experience" of his life.[16] In October 1992, Traficante was indicted on nine misdemeanor counts for campaign finance violations related to over $100,000 in cash contributions kept in a safe deposit box and to ethics violations for failing to disclose his ownership in a company called Collaborators, Inc.[17] Traficante maintained his innocence, refused to resign and charged the attorney general, who was a Democrat, with playing politics. A few weeks later, promising an audit of city finances and "buoyed" by the public "anger over a corruption scandal in City Hall," the Democrats won a six-to-three majority on the city council.[18] It was the first time the Democrats had a majority on the city council since 1980, and it was a majority large enough to override any veto by Traficante.

While trying to defend his reputation, Traficante had to address the city's unraveling finances. After two years of avoiding pay raises for the unions, personnel costs were set to rise by millions in the next fiscal year. Saying that "the hat has literally run out of rabbits," Traficante pulled out a proposed tax increase of $2.39, or 6.4 percent.[19] However, Democrats now controlled the city council and were determined to show they were "very fiscally conservative." After "closed door party caucus meetings," city council Democrats reduced the increase to $1.95, or 5.3 percent, but it was not without controversy. After years of complaining that Traficante wasn't tough on the unions and that city officials were some of the "highest paid in the state," the Democrats decided to eliminate longevity bonuses and require a 25 percent co-share for health insurance for all city administrators and Traficante's political appointees. The Democrats decided to target the city hall employees' association because it had been "nurtured by Republican mayors' political patronage" and had not been officially certified by the State Labor Relations Board as a union. However, the association representing city hall workers and Traficante said it was illegal because "everyone in City Hall but the mayor" was considered a member of the city hall employees' association, and no changes to their compensation could made contrary to their existing contractual agreement. Democrats countered that the situation was unethical since if all city hall employees were union members, it meant that city solicitors and directors who negotiated with the city hall employees' association were negotiating with an organization to which they belonged regarding the raises they would be receiving. Democrats filed a complaint with the Ethics Commission, and the association filed a grievance. An arbitrator agreed with the association, and when Traficante appeared reluctant to appeal the decision, the Democrats on the city council hastily typed a resolution and engaged in "a series of extraordinary parliamentary moves" to appeal the arbitrator's decision to court. However, when a judge upheld the arbitration decision, the Democrats capitulated, and Traficante had to borrow money to pay for the restored pay and benefits of these administrators. A year later, the Ethics Commission dismissed the Democrats' complaint "without comment." It would not be until 1999, after further litigation and negotiation, that city hall administrators and city solicitors would be excluded from the union for city hall employees.[20]

This was not the only act of independence by the activist Democratic city council majority. On a party line vote, the Democrat-controlled city council initiated its investigation with a forensic audit overseen by a Boston lawyer who was a former federal Justice Department official. The audit eventually revealed a "significant pattern of contract and purchasing abuses" in which Traficante's administration "routinely circumvented bidding procedures" involving city contracts for sewer, schools, landscaping, tree trimming and road paving, which, at times, benefited Traficante's campaign contributors.[21] In one instance, one sewer contractor, who happened to be Traficante's fifth-largest donor, was convicted of padding his bills to the city. This city vendor had repeatedly received "no bid" contracts from the Board of Contract and Purchase, on which Traficante and his appointees constituted a majority. Although Traficante admitted it was a "major mistake" to permit this campaign contributor to win no-bid sewer contracts, he did not think there was anything improper about seeking campaign donations from city vendors, saying that he depended "on contributions to run my campaigns." He also adamantly denied that he was "corrupt person" and "lashed out" at a major newspaper for supposed inaccuracies in its reporting on the whole scandal.[22]

The forensic audit was not the only audit that troubled Traficante. The Democrats on the city council selected a new firm to audit the city's finances after complaining that a leading member of the prior firm had contributed to Traficante's campaign. This new auditing firm discovered a deficit of $9.0 million in the sewer fund and $11.4 million in the city's general fund. Millions in sewer fund revenues had been spent on daily city operations. In the "short term," this practice had kept "a lid on the property tax rate," but in the long term, it left a "giant hole" in the city's finances.[23] The Traficante administration blamed the prior auditing firm for not realizing the problem.

Despite this terrible financial news, Traficante proposed a budget for 1994 that did not raise taxes. A few weeks earlier, he had announced he was seeking reelection.

The 1994 mayoral election would prove to be Traficante's most difficult mayoral campaign. He would face city council president Michael Sepe, who was making the city hall scandals a key part of his campaign. Furthermore, a few months after the Rhode Island Supreme Court allowed Traficante's own statements to be used against him as evidence, Traficante plead guilty to willfully failing to report $115,000 in campaign contributions and to nine misdemeanor counts for filing false documents with Board of Elections and the Ethics Commission. He was put on probation and paid a fine.[24]

However, in his battle to stay in office, Traficante still had some advantages. As a "strong mayor" under the home rule charter with the powers of patronage, he could draw on support, financial or otherwise, from city vendors and city hall employees, the two key pillars of the Republican machine that had ruled Cranston for three decades. In addition to this, Traficante had the support of two additional bases of support: the public employee unions and the elderly. The public employee unions were possibly the strongest interest group in Cranston, while the elderly represented the largest demographic group of voters.

As for labor, unlike prior Republican mayors whose relationship with labor could be strained at times, Traficante enjoyed a cooperative relationship with labor unions, and they had endorsed him in his mayoral elections.[25] In 1994, Traficante vowed to eliminate all funding for Cranston's volunteer firefighters because they were allegedly unreliable. After a century of true public service, Traficante believed it was "time to go" for these volunteer firefighter companies, while Sepe supported their funding.[26] The elimination of the volunteer firefighter companies had been a goal of the firefighters' union since 1980, when Mayor Edward DiPrete refused to eliminate them, believing these volunteers were "worth their weight in gold."[27]

As for the elderly, they constituted about 25 percent of the city's population, which was a very high percentage compared to the national average. In general, Rhode Island had a large elderly population because economic stagnation had led to younger members of the population leaving the state for better economic opportunities elsewhere. Cranston's high percentage was also due, in part, to the number of subsidized senior housing projects located in the city, which had been created under the auspices of Cranston Housing Authority or other federal programs. The seniors of these manors did not pay property taxes directly, desired city services and were reliable

Despite his own illegalities involving campaign finances, Mayor Traficante remained in office because of support from the elderly due to his multimillion-dollar senior center.

voters. Traficante charmed and catered to them with a multimillion-dollar senior center and senior-oriented programs and won their loyal support. Immediately after the announcement of Traficante's guilty plea, a reporter decided that the senior center would be a "good place to check the political health" of Traficante, and after interviewing various senior citizens, he concluded the article with one senior citizen saying, "He did a little thing, so big deal. I'll vote for him. There's worse crooks than him around."[28]

The campaign of 1994 concluded with Traficante being reelected with 56 percent of the vote and the Republicans regaining control of the city council. However, one bright spot for the Democrats was that their proposed amendments to the city charter had nearly all passed by margins larger than that by which Traficante had been reelected. These amendments allowed for the recall of elected officials; permitted voter initiative; placed term limits on elected officials, including the mayor; and gave to the city council control over the Board of Contract and Purchase. Cranston voters were giving Traficante a second chance, but they were not taking any more chances on having a "strong mayor" form of government lead to further scandals.

Crisis

Traficante did not enjoy his victory for long. After persevering through one of the two worst things that could befall a mayor—a corruption scandal—he now had to face the other thing mayors most feared: skyrocketing tax increases. Traficante admitted that "the city had been living on borrowed time for several years" by "putting off inevitable tax increases by refinancing the city's debt." The city had borrowed money supported by tax anticipation notes, a "perpetual deficit funding mechanism." The city had only been making interest payments on this debt, and now a $9 million "balloon payment" was due in the next year while the city's bond rating was approaching the level where the state could take over Cranston's finances. Due to these financial problems, Traficante, who during his reelection campaign had "committed to holding the line on taxes," was now proposing a $5.21 property tax increase, which would raise the tax rate by 13.4 percent to $44.00 per $1,000.00. Pastore, the city council minority leader, reminded the public that the Democrats had warned "that Traficante had mortgaged the city's financial future to win reelection" and explained that the "tax increase" was the "culmination of years of imprudent financial and accounting practices."

The tax increase was not stopped by hundreds of angry taxpayers who came to budget hearings to denounce the tax increase and to demand health care co-shares from city employees and a reduction in their retirement benefits. Instead, it was reduced when the Rhode Island auditor general, using his power under state law, refused to grant Cranston permission to raise its taxes higher than a 9.4 percent increase. On a party-line vote, the Republican-controlled city council complied with the auditor general's decision by approving the lower tax increase and balanced the budget by reducing the amount the city would pay into its troubled pension fund and to pay its debt.[29]

The following year was even worse. A new audit showed that the city's deficit had grown to $5 million and was continuing to grow because the previous year's budget had been based on optimistic revenue projections. In his proposed budget for 1996, Traficante tried to emphasize that he was making cuts similar to downsizing private sector companies, when he announced that the city was engaging in its "first large scale work force reduction" by eliminating twenty municipal positions, mostly in city hall, due in part to the implementation of a more efficient computer system. However, these twenty positions constituted less than 5 percent of the city's payroll, and while he was laying off these workers, he was increasing spending by $8.6 million. Furthermore, because of a property revaluation, the size of the tax increase was "camouflaged." However, how much property taxes were increasing for homeowners would not go unnoticed.[30]

Since the previous revaluation, twelve years earlier, a real estate boom in the 1980s had caused residential property values to double or triple, but the value of commercial property had not increased a great deal. As a result of the revaluation, the tax burden was shifted even more onto homeowners in a city that was already overly dependent on the property taxes of residential homeowners. Homeowners in some neighborhoods saw their property taxes grow by over 80 percent. The breaking point for some taxpayers had been reached. A "Boston Tea Party sentiment was in the air." An organization called Cranston United Taxpayers (CUT) was formed, and about six hundred angry residents met at a hall for a rally. When the fire department tried to close down the rally because of overcrowding, the taxpayers spontaneously marched on city hall and attended a city council meeting at which the "emotional crowd," in a "frenzy," shouted down the mayor and lambasted city officials. To some it was "mob rule."[31]

When these taxpayers called for reopening contracts to stop pay raises, end longevity bonuses and require employees to pay a share for their healthcare insurance, Traficante responded by getting the police and firefighters' unions to renegotiate their contracts so that they gave up a pay raise but kept their benefits intact. This is the usual result of negotiating for concessions with public employee unions. CUT members objected to the continuation of the benefits, and the city council unanimously and without discussion rejected Traficante's deals. While the city council, despite a Republican majority, promised further cuts, Traficante promised to "stand up against the City Council and against the public" to "fight for city services that affect quality of life," such as education, recreation and senior services. At another city council hearing, one thousand residents showed up, some of whom "railed against public employees," including "their free health insurance, 17 paid holidays" and their longevity bonuses. At another hearing, a taxpayer offered up the deed to his house because he could not afford the property taxes, saying, "Sell it and split it up between Mayor Traficante and his friends."

Eventually, the city council, on a party-line vote, trimmed the budget by $5 million, although some of this cut was done by postponing paying down the deficit. The tax increase was reduced and a large homestead exemption adopted. CUT vowed to stay active but eventually faded, as did the public's anger when city politicians managed to avoid a tax increase in subsequent years. Although CUT has vanished, this episode in Cranston history would always be remembered as the "Great Tax Revolt of 1996."[32]

Crisis

The Great Tax Revolt was fueled not just by high taxes but also by the disparity in pay and benefits between private sector and public sector employees. This gap, which favored public sector employees, had arisen gradually over decades as global economic forces abroad and less union friendly public policies at home caused private sector compensation to be scaled back, while public sector compensation stayed the same or grew in union-friendly states like Rhode Island. Changing economics caused a change in politics. Traficante, who had enjoyed a cooperative relationship with public employee unions, now began to seek more reductions in their compensation packages and an increase in management rights. In 1995, he got the laborers' union to agree to eliminate longevity bonuses for new hires while also making these new hires pay a 20 percent co-share for health insurance. In the spring of 1996, he had the city council revise the civil service regulations so that he could lay off city hall employees without taking seniority into account in order to maximize savings from such layoffs. Although it angered the union and worried the Democrats since it increased Traficante's power, Republicans saw the change as "revolutionary" because it made "city government more like private business." This achievement would be negotiated away by Traficante's successor in 2000. In the summer of 1996, Traficante was able to get the city hall employees' union to agree to eliminate longevity bonuses for all of its members while requiring new hires to pay a 20 percent co-share for health insurance. The landscape had changed. However, it did not change for the police and firefighters' unions because they had the benefit of more favorable labor laws, such as binding arbitration.

Traficante's efforts to reduce union benefits did not satisfy CUT members, even though Traficante tried to explain the "difficulty of changing the tide of many decades of union gains."[33] To add to Traficante's woes, Cranston Print Works, after nearly two centuries of operation, decided to close its manufacturing plant in Cranston due to high costs associated with workers compensation and unemployment insurance. That same year, Davol, a large manufacturer that had located to Cranston in 1970, decided to close its factory, also citing high costs. On election day, Traficante suffered a "stinging defeat" when the Democrats took every seat on the city council except one: the seat representing the Third Ward, where Traficante's senior center was located. Even a first-time Democratic candidate for city council, who was a law school student, had defeated a veteran Republican city councilman presumed to be Traficante's heir apparent.[34]

Like a proud athlete after a big loss, Traficante did not accept defeat but instead saw it "as a challenge" to overcome. He spoke of seeking reelection in 1998 and, in the final months of 1996, had the lame duck city council approve significant legislation. Traficante, the old math-teacher-turned-wizard of fiscal expediency and budgetary gimmicks, still had a few more lessons in municipal finance to show to the public.

For years, Cranston had been plagued by an unfunded police and fire pension fund, but the speed at which it was growing under Traficante was startling. In 1989, the unfunded pension liability was $53 million. Three years later, in 1992, it was $82 million, and two years later, in 1994, it was $133 million. The city examined various options. One option was to reduce pension benefits, such as requiring a minimum retirement age or reducing cost of living adjustments, but these changes would be hard to achieve because of the opposition of the police and firefighters' unions. Another option was for the city to increase its contribution to the pension fund by fully funding it rather than just contributing enough to pay the benefits of current retirees, but this would require a significant tax increase at a time when taxes were already spiking and taxpayers were already angry. As a result, Traficante decided to maintain the existing pension benefits for all police officers and firefighters in order to win their support for a proposal to transfer newly hired and junior police officers and firefighters into a state-administered pension plan.

Under a state-administered pension plan, the city would be required to fully fund these benefits at actuarial required levels, but the newly hired and junior police officers and firefighters would be required to contribute 10 percent of their pay into the pension fund as well. Under this plan, police and firefighters would receive largely the same pension benefits as they would have under the city-managed pension plan.[35] The Rhode Island General Assembly passed the necessary legislation in 1996, and the city council passed the needed ordinances as well, "without debate."[36] The Traficante administration claimed that these changes would "get rid of this hideous unfinanced liability."[37] However, it had not solved the problem of the unfunded pension liability for those employees and retirees remaining under the city-managed pension system. In fact, it made it worse.

Unbeknownst to the city council, these ordinances increased the pension benefits of those police and firefighters under the city's pension plan. Police and firefighters under the city pension system, including those already retired, would for the first time be guaranteed a minimum 3 percent cost of living increase in their pensions annually.[38] When one city council member raised questions about the proposed ordinances at an earlier meeting, Traficante's director of administration affirmed that "there is nothing new in these ordinances." Years later, a former attorney general would find that the city council had been "presented with misinformation" when it voted on these ordinances.[39] Although the Traficante administration could obfuscate, it could not prevent the unfunded pension liability from growing. When Traficante left office two years later, it stood at $171 million, and it would remain the "city's most dangerous long-term financial problem" until it, along with other problems, brought the city to the brink of bankruptcy about six years later.[40]

In December 1996, after a year of reviewing the possibility of the City leasing its sewer system to a private company, Traficante proposed, and the city council approved, a twenty-five-year lease agreement with a private company to manage the Cranston sewer system. In return, Cranston received an upfront payment of approximately $48 million with which Traficante paid off the city's sewer-related debt, erased debt owed the general fund by the sewer fund and turned an operating deficit into a surplus of about $6 million. Thus, the sewer system, which had generated so much debate and financial trouble in the past, was now used to momentarily alleviate the city's ongoing financial crisis. Relying in part on proceeds from the privatization of the sewer plant, in the following year, Traficante proposed a tax rate of $31.98 per $1,000.00, an eleven-cent decrease in the tax rate. Traficante claimed it was a sign that that city's finances were improving, while his critics called it "smoke and mirrors" and stated that "nothing had changed" since the funds from the sewer privatization were just a "one time windfall to the city to correct its past sins."[41] The city council further lowered the tax rate to $31.74 per $1,000.00, an approximate 1 percent decrease in the property tax rate.

Traficante seemed to be making another comeback until some of the problems that had plagued his administration in the past seemed to be returning. The finance director resigned after he was "unable to provide detailed answers to questions about the budget and the tardy audit." The city's bond rating dropped again. In the fall of 1997, the city's treasurer and director of computer services were indicted for bribery for accepting kickbacks in return for giving computer service contracts to the city's former purchasing agent in the early 1990s.[42] A newspaper editorial was dumbfounded at what seemed "to be encouraging the corruption" in Cranston and speculated about a "lack of proper internal controls" or the "poor leadership" and "poor example" set by Traficante.[43] A few weeks later, Traficante announced that he would not seek reelection. Traficante, the former star athlete, said he did not "want to be one of those players that stays one season too long." Even his supporters agreed it was "time for the mayor to move on."[44]

In the 1998 election, the Democrats enjoyed what some believed was the "greatest victory" that they would "ever have" in Cranston as voters sent a clear message to the Republicans to "get out" by electing only Democrats to the city council and electing state senator John O'Leary as mayor in a landslide, with 65 percent of the vote. It was the worst showing for a Republican mayoral candidate in the history of Cranston. Along with these historic changes, the voters approved changes to the city charter, which reduced the mayor's term from four years to two years, while requiring the mayor to obtain the advice and consent of the city council for the appointment of department heads. The Republican machine had collapsed, and the "strong mayor" form of government had been changed to one where the mayor's powers were more limited.[45]

Leaving the mayor's office did not mean Traficante would leave politics. Traficante went on to become a lobbyist for the laborers' union, with which he had enjoyed "very good relationship" as mayor.[46] When the city's finances were in disarray in 2002, Mayor O'Leary and Traficante blamed each other for the mess. In 2004, Traficante battled with Mayor Stephen P. Laffey after they had a falling out. In that same year, Traficante was elected with just 52 percent of the vote to represent the Fifth Ward on the Cranston School Committee after he defeated a little-known and under-funded opponent. The voters had either forgiven him once again or had simply forgotten about the problems of the past. Eventually, he became chairman of the school committee and led the school committee to court in order to obtain more education funding from the city at the time it was headed by Mayor Michael T. Napolitano. The school committee lost the suit and its appeal to the Rhode Island Supreme Court. As a result, the school committee reduced or eliminated various sports, music and gifted programs and today owes the city a debt of approximately $6.7 million for its past overspending.

When Traficante was inducted into the Cranston Hall of Fame, it was not without controversy. His critics pointed to the corruption scandals of his administration and his guilty pleas to campaign finance misdemeanors, while supporters pointed to the city services he had provided to the youth and the elderly during his mayoral tenure. Whether or not one agrees that Traficante belongs in a hall of fame, there should be little debate that he exemplified Cranston's governance for the last quarter century, with its mixture of quality city services, numerous tot parks, comprehensive senior programs, high taxes, financial troubles and scandals.

Crisis

John O'Leary

1999–2003

For nearly four decades, Cranston Republicans controlled the mayor's office. The man who ended this political dynasty was John O'Leary. He was an education administrator at the University of Rhode Island. He served for one term in the state senate when he lived in Providence during the early 1980s. After moving to Cranston, he was elected to the state senate in 1990 and climbed to the rank of deputy majority leader. In 1998, when the likely Democratic nominee for mayor, city council president Peter T. Pastore Jr., made a surprise announcement that he would not run for mayor, O'Leary emerged as the leading candidate. Weary of high taxes and leery of scandals, voters elected O'Leary in a landslide, with 65 percent of the vote, and the Democrats won every seat on the city council. As Democrats crowed, an exiting Republican councilman warned Democrats to "be careful what you wish for."[47]

In his first budget, O'Leary saw that the city had a structural deficit because expenses were growing faster than revenues. He noted that the city's spending was increasing at 5 percent per year, while the city's revenues were growing at only 2 percent per year. As a result, deficits would arise in the next two years. O'Leary admonished that "we must learn from the past, not repeat it." However, rather than proposing a tax increase, he proposed to dip into the city's surplus—the rainy day fund—which at the time stood at approximately $10 million. O'Leary justified the use of the rainy day fund as a stopgap measure to "buy time" for him time to implement his long-term plans. But O'Leary also admitted to another motivation, which was less farsighted. O'Leary stated, "I would have a hard time telling people I have $10 million in a rainy day fund and that we are going to raise taxes."[48]

While voters were pleased with a tax freeze, the school committee was dissatisfied because it had requested an 8.4 percent increase, but O'Leary had only given it a 4 percent increase. The school committee talked about various cuts to extracurricular programs. Some called them scare tactics. The city council eventually increased the school budget, but it was not enough for the school committee, so the committee threatened legal action, as well as cuts to middle school sports and bus routes. To end the dispute for that year, O'Leary gave the schools an additional $500,000 and sought a good faith effort by the School Department to consolidate various school and city services, but no results came of these efforts.

In the next year, the school committee sought a 7 percent increase. Once again, the School Department was disappointed when O'Leary proposed a budget that only increased the school budget by 5 percent and did not raise taxes. When O'Leary announced that the rainy day fund had not been needed to balance the prior year's budget, some called for spending the rainy day fund to provide more money to the schools. O'Leary's director of administration labeled that proposal a "band-aid solution," which would only "double the problem in the year after." A school committee member retorted that it was not a band-aid solution when O'Leary had proposed it in the prior year. When the school committee threatened legal action again, O'Leary encouraged it and noted that no other department had its budget increased by 10 percent in the previous two years. Protesters with signs saying, "The surplus is ours, use it for the schools!" marched in front of city hall, but the city council adopted O'Leary's budget.[49]

While O'Leary was haggling with the School Department, he was trying to come to an understanding with the police union. When O'Leary took office, both the firefighters' union and the police union were in arbitration. Leaders of Cranston United Taxpayers aired rumors that O'Leary had promised favorable contracts to the police and firefighters' unions in return for their endorsements in the election. O'Leary denied it. However, within a few months of entering office, O'Leary reached a five-year deal with the police union. The deal was killed by city council leaders because they believed that the Cranston Police Department was already well paid and that the only way to "control taxes is to control salaries" because "most of the costs of government are labor related."[50]

O'Leary tried again later that same year by proposing a five-year deal with a few more changes. Once again, the city council president Kevin J. McAllister opposed it by saying that the deal would "perpetuate the same labor policies and fiscal policies that almost led to the city's bankruptcy three years ago."[51] One area of contention was the "strict seniority rules" in the police contract that, according to Cranston police chief James Abbott, did "not reward hard work" because it suggested to "officers early on that no matter how hard they work, no matter how dedicated they are," it would have "no bearing on how they are going to move through the department." Instead, Police Chief Abbott wanted policies to be based in part on "merit, experience and work ethic." A police management consultant noted that the police "chief has very little authority to manage the department, due to seniority rules and lack of management rights in the contract," and concluded that the police department was "run by the union."[52] When the city council split evenly, with the approval of the contract coming down to one swing vote, the police union backed out of the deal.

A few months later, O'Leary tried a third time. This time it was a six-year deal slightly modified to address a few issues related to seniority in order to win over the swing vote on the city council. A few weeks later, the police union contract passed on a five-to-four vote. However, a few weeks before the vote, one of the councilmen who had opposed the police contract was denied the endorsement of the Cranston Democratic Party in favor of the president of the police union of a neighboring town. This brought objections from city council president Kevin McAllister, who accused the police and firefighters' unions of a "blatant attempt" to "hijack the City Council."[53] Subsequently, in the Democratic primary for city council, the police union president circulated a memo to his members saying that the endorsed Democrat was "committed to support any issues which impact us, including our next contract."[54] The Democrat, who was endorsed by the police union, won the primary and went on to serve as chairman of the Finance Committee.

A few weeks after the primary, the city council decided by a vote of seven to two not to appeal a binding arbitration decision on the firefighters' contract. O'Leary's director of administration gestured to the thirty firefighters in attendance and said it was time to "negotiate with these people," while President McAllister, who was leaving office, accused O'Leary of "collusion" with the firefighters' union.[55] While the Democrats were divided on unions, the voters were excited about no tax increases or scandals for two years. As a result, the Democrats swept all the seats on the city council. On election night, a councilwoman declared, "The Republicans are dead in this city."[56] But within two years, the financial health of the city would be seen as gravely ill and the prospects of Cranston Republicans as alive and well.

In the following year, O'Leary began to make changes in his fiscal policy. First, while focusing on the positive, O'Leary proposed his first property tax increase of 2.6 percent. Second, O'Leary proposed legislation that would have allowed Cranston to take out a pension obligation bond for the city's unfunded police and fire pension liability. The money from this bond would have been invested in the stock market to pay retirees and bondholders. This approach carried a risk because if the investments did not grow as fast as needed, taxpayers would have to pay both the retirees and the bondholders. Although the bill passed the General Assembly, Republican governor Lincoln Almond vetoed it on the basis that it would just replace one financial debt with another.

At this time, Republicans began to attack O'Leary for the tardiness of the city audits. O'Leary's director of administration explained that while O'Leary had "professionalized the city fiscal services," the delay was due to problems in the computer system they had inherited.[57] Less than ten days later, O'Leary's director of administration, a man he had heavily relied on, resigned. There was something brewing. But before it would be revealed, O'Leary's top economic development project came to fruition at the site of the former Narragansett Brewery. After nearly two decades of disappointment, a retail plaza was opened. The day after this high point for O'Leary, it would be downhill for him and the city's bond rating.

In October 2001, O'Leary suddenly announced that the city's $10.1 million rainy day fund was gone. The city council had never been told of the situation. O'Leary explained that some of the rainy day fund had gone to pay pension costs and other operating expenses.[58] O'Leary blamed his former director of administration for bad information on the status of the rainy day fund by saying, "You have been misled and I have been misled," while disclosing that the rainy day fund had been a factor in his director's resignation a few months earlier. In response, the former director of the administration pointed to the finance department. Eventually, the finance director said, "I made a mistake" and explained that "there was confusion that the rainy day fund was locked away somewhere and nobody could ever touch it without an act of God."[59] This was the beginning of what one major newspaper headlined as the "Cranston Financial Crisis."

After the Tax Revolt of 1996, the O'Leary administration and the city council were anxious to avoid a tax increase, but cost cutting fell short, and revenue projections had been too rosy. For instance, in the budget adopted in 2001, the city assumed that it would have a 100 percent tax collection rate. The audits, which would have given a warning to city officials, were not done on time. Without the outside audits to show the shortfalls, the administration relied on internally generated documents that appeared to show budget surpluses when, in fact, the rainy day fund was being used up. As a result, in the fiscal year 2000, the city ended with a deficit of $5.5

million. In the fiscal year 2001, the city ended with a deficit of $10.2 million. Unwittingly, they had spent the entire rainy day fund.

O'Leary had not raised any alarms earlier, and in fact, during his first three budget addresses, he had asserted that the city had $10 million in its rainy day fund because "he was trying to paint a positive picture of the city." Now, in the fiscal year 2002, there was a projected $11.5 million budget deficit, and the usually positive O'Leary could not help but call it a "crisis situation." Republicans accused O'Leary of misleading the public and mismanaging finances. O'Leary blamed former mayor Michael Traficante from whom said he had inherited a structural deficit and unfunded pension liability. Traficante said O'Leary had squandered his inheritance—the rainy day fund—and that O'Leary's legacy would be of "lies, mismanagement and misrepresentations."[60]

As the audits were produced, Cranston's bond rating began to dive. One credit agency said that things had "fallen apart" in Cranston. O'Leary thought the solution was a pension obligation bond, but it died in the legislature when the auditor general expressed disapproval. Calls for a state takeover of city finances were made by Republicans and some Democrats. Fear of a state takeover caused a wave of retirements in the police and fire departments out of fear that their pensions could be reduced. To stave off such a takeover, in 2002, O'Leary proposed a budget that raised taxes by 10.4 percent, level funded the schools and budgeted millions in union concessions. The auditor general was not satisfied and said that O'Leary's budget was not balanced, relied too much on taxes and needed more union concessions, which to him did not mean deferrals. In the midst of this storm, the city council decided to oust city council president Joseph DeLorenzo over some controversies surrounding his former position in the office of secretary of state, but a judge blocked the ouster. This melodrama was followed by a public hearing attended by nine hundred residents "venting venom" and yelling, "Where's the rainy day fund!" One credit rating agency had seen enough and dropped the city's bond rating to junk status. The credit rating agency said that the city's recovery plan was "too vague, too little, almost too late" and stated that the proposed union concessions included deferrals that were "only solving the problem temporarily." O'Leary had hoped he had more "time" and said the "negative publicity" had "hastened the downgrade," but as always, he looked for something positive and said "it's always darkest before the dawn." It would get darker still.[61]

The city council passed an amended budget that increased taxes by 11.5 percent and used up most of the pension fund that had been built up over nearly two decades to balance the budget. Under the city council's budget, the assets in the pension fund would decrease from $20.8 million to $4.5

million, and the pension fund would have been only 2 percent funded by July 2003. Stephen P. Laffey, the Republican mayoral candidate, compared what the city council had done to taking money out of "your 401(k) to pay off credit card bills." But the city council "had achieved their goal of fending off a state takeover," a goal shared by O'Leary.[62]

After using pension funds to balance the budget, O'Leary negotiated a series of union contracts. All city unions gave up raises in the first year of their contracts but in most cases got raises into 2005. The city hall workers' union, laborers' union and crossing guards' union also got no-layoff clauses in their contracts. The firefighters got an increase in longevity bonuses and a September 11 holiday. Laffey said the contracts were "indicative of a recovery plan that pushes the city's financial crisis from the present to the near future" and called it a "great plan if the world ends in three months." Shortly thereafter, it became known that another credit rating agency had downgraded the city's bond rating to junk bond status. O'Leary did not notify the public or the city council until a week after it occurred, causing Council President DeLorenzo to say, "We've been kept in the dark and I'm sick and tired of it." A few days after this downgrade was publicized, O'Leary stunned Democrats by deciding not to seek reelection. While acknowledging mistakes, he placed most of the blame on prior Republican administrations. He also blamed local legislators for failing to pass a pension obligation bond and accused the auditor general of scare tactics.[63]

In his last few months, O'Leary also had to address a controversy surrounding the public works garage. In a complicated series of transactions, the city had created a nonprofit corporation that then issued debt to purchase a public works garage so as to lease it back to the city; this avoided the requirement that the debt be approved by the voters. This nonprofit purchased the land for the garage from a company that was owned by a business partner of the city solicitor. This company bought the land and sold it to the nonprofit all in one day, for a gain of $475,000. The city then contracted with another company owned by this same business partner to maintain the building for $40,000 a year, a building that housed the city's building maintenance department.[64] When O'Leary came under fire for this whole episode, he criticized the newspaper coverage for casting a "negative light on the project" and explained that he had delegated the work on the project to his former director of administration. His former director of administration responded that O'Leary had made all the decisions and criticized O'Leary for "being unwilling to take responsibility for his actions" and for taking "credit for all of the good and none of the bad."[65]

Crisis

Under Mayor O'Leary, Cranston's public works garage produced controversy.

When the bond rating dropped again, O'Leary had to fend off another state takeover attempt, this time led by Mayor-elect Laffey. O'Leary denounced Laffey and others for saying that "the sky is falling and putting out horrible lies." He called them "some really sick people, some really evil people" and "accused the news media of inaccurately reporting finances." Laffey defended himself by saying that he was basically repeating what the "auditor general and the rating agencies" were stating.[66]

Just before he left office, O'Leary had to endure one last media storm. When he first took office, O'Leary had called the severance packages Mayor Traficante's departing employees received a "rip off" because they had been able to accrue a large number of vacation days, sick days and compensatory time. The total severance package for these eighteen employees was $380,386. As a result, O'Leary placed "several strict restrictions on the severance payouts," and in April 1999, the city council approved the policy. But as O'Leary's appointees were leaving, it came to light that O'Leary had unilaterally changed the policy he had first adopted to make it easier for employees to build up compensatory time for attending meetings outside normal business hours. O'Leary's fourteen outgoing appointees received $210,881. He had changed his mind on the issue because he had "learned that it costs money to run the city."[67]

After leaving public office, O'Leary oversaw urban schools for the Catholic Church and eventually became an education administrator at the University of Rhode Island. O'Leary "virtually disappeared after his tumultuous term as mayor," but his successor and most vocal critic, Laffey, kept his administration in the spotlight and made it synonymous with "mismanagement" to the public.[68] Democrats took him to task as well. The Democratic Party chairman criticized O'Leary for not taking his advice and called O'Leary's last budget "terrible " and "not fiscally sound." Another party officer said that O'Leary and his administration were simply "asleep at the switch and afraid to face reality."[69] They had cheered him; now they flayed him, a likeable man who had "never tried to intentionally hurt the city."[70]

As O'Leary left office, he spoke of his "pride" in the economic development that occurred in Cranston while he was mayor. However, as he noted in his inaugural address, "some will measure my success in terms of improved tax rates and bond ratings." For them, there were no apologies. He acknowledged that some things should have been "done differently" but said "human beings are not perfect." He left city hall "holding" his "head high," but the city's bond rating was as low as could be.[71]

STEPHEN P. LAFFEY

2003–2007

Being the mayor of Cranston can be a high-profile position, but no mayor garnered so much publicity in so short a time as Stephen P. Laffey. During his childhood, his parents' attention was focused on the needs of his troubled siblings, but he was focused on being successful. He earned an MBA from Harvard, became a stockbroker, excelled at stock picking and eventually became president of an investment banking firm in Tennessee. After the firm was sold, he returned to Cranston. With Cranston in the midst of a financial crisis, Laffey, who had always had political aspirations, felt a calling from God to run for mayor.[72] He ran as a financial expert who would solve Cranston's financial crisis. His Democratic opponent was Aram Garabedian. Garabedian had been a fixture in local Cranston politics for decades by running successfully for various offices under different party banners and was an owner of the Warwick Mall. In debates, Laffey labeled Garabedian a "career politician," while Garabedian waved an article discussing Laffey's "abrupt departure" from his Tennessee investment banking firm due to "personality conflicts."[73] Demanding change, Laffey won with 52 percent of the vote, and the Republicans won three seats on the city council.

Laffey did not wait to be sworn in to make an impact. When a credit rating agency dropped Cranston's bond rating to the lowest in the nation, Laffey urged a state takeover. When Governor Almond was unwilling, Laffey threatened to default on short-term loans coming due in February 2003. Governor Almond did not budge, but Laffey's "inflammatory language" caused a credit rating agency to further drop the city's bond rating.[74] In the waning days of the O'Leary administration, as O'Leary's fourteen appointees were about to leave office with $210,881 in severance pay, mostly for compensatory time, Laffey tried to block these payments, saying, "The people who crashed the *Titanic* into an iceberg didn't get comp time when they fled in lifeboats," but a judge denied his request.[75]

In his first inaugural address, Laffey gave a hint of how polarizing a figure he would become. He stated, "There are two real and distinct blocs of people in any city." Some had a "very narrow interest," and then there were "those with a broad interest." He would be "fighting for" those with the broader interest.[76] When he entered office, the city had a deficit of $11.9 million, was spending down the pension fund and had only about a month to pay back $18 million in short-term loans. As a result, Laffey first stopped draining the pension fund, which was down to about $10 million. Second, Laffey pursued legislation to allow Cranston to borrow money backed by the state aid it received. However, in order to win passage, legislators indicated that Cranston needed to pass a supplemental tax. As a result, Laffey proposed, and the city council adopted, a 12.8 percent supplemental property tax increase, which eliminated the city's prior deficits. With this tax increase, Cranston taxpayers would see their property taxes increase by 25 percent in one year. After the desired legislation was enacted, the city was able to take out low-interest, short-term loans and avoid default.

Raising taxes was the easy part of the solution. Taxpayers called for cuts to the compensation of city employees. Laffey promised $11 million in cuts. At a public forum in March 2003, Laffey unveiled $11 million in cuts, which included the elimination of the crossing guards' program but consisted primarily of a reduction to the city's contribution to the pension fund and a decrease in the school committee's proposal to increase the school budget. Laffey also proposed reductions to the pensions of police officers and firefighters who had retired prior to 1996 by eliminating their minimum 3-percent-per-year cost of living increase and by eliminating the 5 percent increase given to retired police officers and firefighters when they reached age fifty-five. His proposals garnered much applause from residents, but the union leaders called it grandstanding. Laffey claimed that the pension benefits he wanted eliminated had been a gift to police and firefighters granted through a city ordinance in 1996, and thus, the benefits could be rescinded by ordinance. The police and firefighters' unions argued that these pension benefits were covered by contracts as a result of collective bargaining. When dozens of firefighters spoke out in opposition to Laffey's proposal, the city council tabled the ordinances. But after a newspaper published the phone numbers of city council members, urging residents to call, the city council voted in favor of repealing the pension benefits. The matter went into litigation.

As for the crossing guards' program, it had originally been created in 1964 by a lame duck city council at its last meeting and had a small cost of $40,000 to employ thirty-five women. The crossing guard program was included in the school budget until the fiscal year 1975–76, the year that a lengthy teachers' strike occurred. The school committee shifted the cost of the program to the city as a "budgetary protest."[77] In 1976, the city gave the crossing guard union free family health insurance, like all other city employees, but cost was not an issue since much of the personnel costs of the crossing guard program were federally funded through CETA. When federal funds dried up, the program continued with all its benefits intact and stayed unnoticed for years. Under the contract that existed when Laffey became mayor, the crossing guards worked one hour per day for forty weeks, collected unemployment in the summer, got sick days and holidays, received a salary of $8,540 per year and received family health insurance. It was called "the best gig in town."[78] The crossing guards' union stated that it provided a safety service, had a no-layoff clause in its contract and the city could not break a union contract by eliminating the program. However, the public outcry against it was too strong, and the city council eliminated the program from the budget. This dispute also went into litigation.

Regarding the School Department, Laffey proposed to increase the budget by $9 million, which was still $6 million less than what the schools had requested.

Crisis

The School Department noted that Cranston schools outperformed other schools in other urban ring communities while spending less per pupil than these other communities and that the schools had not received funds from the two large tax increases that occurred in 2002 and 2003.

The city council adopted Laffey's budget. Things deteriorated quickly between Laffey and the School Department. Laffey believed that the city's bond rating would have difficulty increasing until the schools stopped deficit spending. He held press conferences stating that the schools had run deficits in their healthcare fund for years. Laffey told the school committee to balance its budget or face legal action. School committee members considered Laffey's actions to be mere antics and said he did not understand that "this is not private industry." Laffey filed an action with the Rhode Island Supreme Court to force the schools to balance their budget but was told to re-file it in Superior Court. The schools filled forty vacancies in the School Department because, in the eyes of school officials, leaving them vacant would have dismantled the school system. As a candidate, Laffey had said, "The waste is not in the schools."[79] Now, Laffey said that "giving money to the school system without demanding discipline is like giving an ATM card to a drug addict to support his habit."[80] Laffey filed a new court action seeking $5 million personally against school committee members for running a deficit. Laffey saw it as a way of holding elected officials accountable for their spending, but one school committee member said it was simply bullying.

Soon thereafter, negotiations between the city council and the school committee broke down over a difference of $3.2 million because the school committee refused to cut programs. The school committee decided to eliminate sports and file a "Caruolo action" in court for $3.2 million. Laffey called it "blackmail."[81] At the same time the school committee was filing its lawsuit, high school students went to city hall to protest the cuts by chanting "no sports, no schools." Laffey, holding his varsity sports jacket in one hand and a bull horn in another, said he had given enough to schools for sports and told the students to go see the school superintendent, who could restore the sports program. The students "yelling and cheering swarmed across the lawn and stormed" the nearby school administration building before they were told to leave.[82] The school committee decided to keep the sports program intact pending its suit. The school committee lost its case, with the judge ruling that the schools had "fallen woefully short" in proving their case. School committee members lamented that it was the beginning of the demise of public education in Cranston because students would now receive "just a very basic education."[83]

The fears of the school committee were misplaced. For all his rhetoric regarding overspending by the school committee, Laffey increased school funding by approximately 40 percent in just four years. However, Laffey did recognize the inherent conflict of having one political body with the autonomy to spend money and the other political body with the sole authority to raise the money. As a result, Laffey proposed that either schools need to send out their own tax bills or cities need to be granted control over school budgets.[84]

Within a few months, after the auditor general noted that the city had a surplus of $7 million rather than $3 million, the schools' prior deficit was forgiven by the city, Laffey withdrew his $5 million lawsuit and the School Department became more forthcoming on sharing its financial information with the city. However, the School Department did not adopt the recommendations of a performance audit, which indicated that the School Committee could save $6 million by adopting such measures as privatizing transportation and food services. These types of changes did not start being implemented until after another court-ordered audit was performed following another failed attempt by the school committee to pursue a Caruolo action later in the decade.

In regards to the crossing guards, Laffey fired them in the summer of 2003, but a judge ordered Laffey to rehire them and called his move "union busting." As this was occurring, Laffey released video surveillance of crossing guards leaving their posts early and city street sweepers sleeping on the job. He got national publicity for this, while the crossing guard union's lawyer said Laffey was just "seeking headlines" and "creating hysteria." When he was criticized for invading privacy rights, Laffey said there was no right to "sleep on the job" and that the public had a right not to be "ripped off." In the end, after all the hoopla, the workers who had been caught sleeping were given a two-week suspension.[85]

After this, Laffey angered the firefighters' union. A performance audit showed that the fire department's staffing should be decreased by 25 percent based on analysis of the size of fire departments in other New England states. The firefighters' union, which had refused to meet with the consultant because he had testified for the city in a prior arbitration, said a reduction in staffing would be illegal because of minimum manning staffing requirements in their contract and that the audit was faulty because it was not limited to comparisons to other Rhode Island cities. Laffey's director of administration responded that the audit should not be limited to comparing Cranston to other Rhode Island cities because Rhode Island was so labor friendly. He also noted that based on the national average, Cranston's fire department would need only 111 firefighters, which meant that Cranston was about 223 percent more expensive than the national average.[86]

At this time, Laffey suffered setbacks in arbitration. Arbitrators found in favor of the police and firefighters' union on Laffey's pension reductions and in favor of the crossing guards on his termination of their program. Laffey appealed to the courts. He stated that when it comes to arbitration, the "deck is stacked against you in Rhode Island," and when firefighters marched in protest in front of city hall, Laffey pulled out his bullhorn and mocked them by asking if this was "a new fitness program."[87]

At this point, the leaders of public employee unions had had enough of Laffey. In 2002, the teachers and police unions had endorsed him. Now unions were going to try and defeat him. The lawyer for the crossing guards' union sent a letter to union members, saying, "From Burrillville to Westerly, weak politicians" are attacking "our wages and benefits" out of "fear of the press if they don't act like Laffey." The plan was to have union members who were Democrats disaffiliate so they could vote in a Republican primary and support another Republican candidate, who was the husband of the crossing guards' union steward. The rhetoric escalated. Laffey was called a liar, a user and a dictator. He called his opponent a puppet of the unions. Applying a Wall Street saying, Laffey called union leaders pigs at the trough and noted, "Pigs get slaughtered." He also borrowed terminology from the Second World War and called politicians who supported public employee unions the equivalent of French collaborators. Laffey's opponent had the "support of every union in the city," while Laffey called his supporters a "rag tag band of revolutionaries" in a taxpayers' revolution.[88]

The war of words almost became physical when, at a city council meeting in which a medical waiver form for injuries suffered on duty was being discussed, the leader of the firefighters' union charged toward Laffey and said, "I'll knock you right out" after Laffey told a firefighter to "please stop" having his wife testify about his injuries. At this same meeting, Laffey and the auditor general "traded bitter words," with the auditor general saying Laffey failed to make cuts and Laffey later saying that the auditor general was just an appointee of the Democrat-controlled legislature.[89]

On primary day, Laffey defeated his union-backed Republican primary opponent in a record-breaking turnout by a margin of three to one. Laffey called it an "earthquake."[90] As one Democrat noted, the union effort had backfired because it had scared people into coming out against them.[91] In the general election, Laffey won with 64 percent of vote, but Democrats retained control of the city council.

At his second inauguration, referencing a popular television commercial of the time, Laffey proclaimed that "taxpayers can rest assured that if the special interests attack" like "barbarians," he would be "there to protect them."[92] After reaching the heights of inflammatory rhetoric, in January 2005, Laffey reached the peak of his success as mayor. A judge ruled that Laffey could fire the crossing guards because a city could not bargain away rights in its charter; thus, the no-layoff clause in the contract was void.[93] A private contractor was hired, and the city saved about $500,000 per year. Although the savings were small in the overall budget, they sent a significant message to public officials about how they could approach public employee unions.

Laffey frequently compared the firing of the crossing guards to President Reagan's firing of the air traffic controllers in 1981. Like the crossing guards, the compensation of these air traffic controllers made up a small portion of the federal budget. However, Reagan's action sent a bold message that put labor unions on the defensive for years. In the decade since the firing of the crossing guards, there has been an erosion in the compensation of public employees through legislation, litigation, regulation and negotiation.[94]

In recent years, the pension benefits and retiree healthcare of state workers and teachers were reduced by legislation.[95] A Superior Court judge decided that a school committee had the legal right to unilaterally reduce the pay and benefits of teachers after a contract was expired. The state commissioner of education required changes to the work schedules of teachers at a failing school. Lastly, Mayor Fung, through negotiation, got the first municipal union to agree to require newly hired employees to join a 401(k) plan. Whether this represents a trend or is an aberration, and whether Laffey was a groundbreaker or an anomaly, remains for the future to decide.[96]

About a week after the crossing guard decision, a credit rating agency raised the city's bond rating out of junk bond status to investment grade. It had required three tax increases under Laffey, the building up of the rainy day fund to $16 million and a move to fully fund the police and fire pension fund. When Laffey left office two years later, the rainy day fund stood at about $20 million, and over the course of the four budgets he prepared, he had funded the pension fund at 99.5 percent of what was recommended by actuaries. As a result, the pension fund had a balance of $49 million and a funding ratio of nearly 20 percent. In 2006, he also began funding the city's other unfunded liability: retiree healthcare for police and firefighters. Although Laffey did not raise taxes in his last two years, and in fact lowered them by 1.5 percent in 2006, he had not solved the structural problem of Cranston's municipal finances, which was that government spending was growing at a faster rate than revenues were growing, the same problem confronting the state and federal governments.

Believing that his mission in Cranston was done, Laffey began to explore other activities, such as having a radio talk show and started to pursue another office, a seat in the U.S. Senate held by an incumbent Republican. In his final two years, Laffey encountered some setbacks. For example, he lost his court case to reduce the pension benefits for police officers and firefighters.[97] Also, Laffey had difficulty working with a city council led by Garabedian. In his first two years as mayor, there was friction between Laffey and the city council, led by Peter Pastore Jr. This friction arose from the irritation that the city council felt from Laffey's lack of consultation with them and his constant communication with the media. The city council criticized Laffey on various issues: his legal expenses, some of which went to the firm of a childhood role model; the hiring of his campaign manager as a summer intern; the city's holiday display, which included pink flamingos; and soundproofing in his office.[98] However, in the crisis atmosphere, the city council had backed Laffey on the major issues.

With the crisis over and with Garabedian as city council president, the city council pursued a variety of court actions, ordinances and charter amendments to check Laffey's powers. Laffey and the city council battled over a variety of topics. The wrangling involved: an increase in school funding, the participation of the city council in union negotiations, promotions in the police department, confirmation of an economic development director, a nearly worthless fire truck, the use of vacant office space, hiring outside legal counsel, automated cameras to catch speeders, privatization of the vehicle maintenance division, claims arising from a flood, a mayoral letter included with tax bills and a permit issued to a concrete plant. It was an exhaustive list that led to almost endless bickering. Laffey did not hide his disdain for the Democrats on the city council. He said that some members on the city council "couldn't run a Del's lemonade stand."[99]

Despite these differences with the city council, Laffey did score some successes. He was able to push the School Department to expel about two hundred students who did not live in Cranston. The city council approved of Laffey's proposed new police station. His administration negotiated and won council approval for three labor contracts that required healthcare co-shares for all employees—in the case of city hall workers, a 20 percent co-share—and introduced health savings accounts in an attempt to control costs. The police union contract also required police officers hired after July 1, 2002, to pay a portion of their retiree health insurance, but it also increased longevity bonuses. When police union leaders complained that Laffey's administration had improperly altered the contract to only gradually increase the pay of younger officers rather than having it immediately increased, Laffey stood firm and referred to the union leadership as "barbarians."[100]

Laffey's race for the U.S. Senate garnered much national attention. In the week leading up to the Republican primary in 2006, his opponent's internal polling showed Laffey "pulling narrowly ahead."[101] On primary day, Laffey garnered more votes than any other candidate ever before in a Republican primary, but it was still a few thousand votes short of his opponent, Lincoln Chafee. Laffey blamed his loss on an influx of non-Republican voters into the primary and the large expenditure of resources by national Republicans to get out votes for his opponent and to air negative personal attack ads on him.[102] Former mayor Michael Traficante, a friend-turned-foe, said Laffey's personality played a role in his loss.

After leaving city hall, Laffey wrote a book about his senatorial campaign, and it was expected that he would run for governor in 2010. However, in the spring of 2009, he announced he was not running for governor and was leaving the state. Despite this announcement, Laffey did not seem at peace with his decision and returned to Rhode Island. A "draft Laffey" movement emerged, but he again declined to run. However, Laffey continued to take speaking engagements, and some believed he would eventually run. In the spring of 2010, he left without public explanation, leaving others to speculate about the reasons for his departure.

Although Laffey never held statewide office, he made a statewide impact. His involvement in Rhode Island politics was brief, but like a "supernova" or a "bolt of political lightening," it made an impression.[103] To his supporters, he was the "savior of Cranston," who was "brilliant, decisive and a courageous friend of the taxpayer," but to his detractors, he had a "massive ego" with a "lust for the limelight" and was "power-mad" with a "messianic complex."[104] His message was polarizing, but even more so was his personality. Eventually, his personality faults overshadowed the merits of his policies. Laffey seemed to combine within himself great talents and great flaws. His talents got him as far he did, and his flaws kept him from going further.

Laffey now resides on a ranch located in the foothills of the Rocky Mountains, where he raises cattle and horses. From there, Laffey can see the peaks of these mountains and, if willing, can contemplate the heights to which his ambitions soared and the rocky path he followed to reach them. But undoubtedly, Laffey's restless spirit will not allow him to find contentment in bucolic serenity. Instead, he will wander to and fro until he finds a controversy he can make his cause.

Crisis

MICHAEL T. NAPOLITANO

2007–2009

There have been many close races for mayor in Cranston, but the closest race, on a percentage basis, occurred in 2006. The winner of that contest was Michael T. Napolitano, who won with 50.11 percent of the vote. Napolitano was a tax lawyer who served as a Cranston municipal court judge. In 2006, he became the Democratic mayoral nominee. He "promised meaningful tax relief" and "help for the city's schools."[105] His Republican opponent was Councilman Allan W. Fung, who had been a strong supporter of Mayor Laffey's policies during the financial crisis. In a variety of ways, Fung tied Napolitano to former Mayor O'Leary. For example, Fung attacked Napolitano for wanting to spend some of the city's $20 million rainy day fund, like O'Leary had done during the city's recent financial crisis. Meanwhile, Napolitano tied Fung to Laffey, who had only carried Cranston by 53 percent in his recent bruising U.S. Senate primary. Also, Napolitano attacked Fung for raising taxes three times with Laffey. Aided by a national Democratic wave, Napolitano won the mayor's race by seventy-two votes.

After taking office, Napolitano first had to contend with a budget containing a significant error. Before Laffey had left office, it had become known that an error had been made in calculating the city's revenues and, as a result, the budget had overestimated revenues by $2 million. However, both Laffey and the city council's auditor still projected a small surplus by the end of the fiscal year. Despite this, at his inauguration, Napolitano still warned of a looming deficit. A month later, after the city council's auditor again concluded there would not be a deficit, Napolitano remained "very, very worried."[106] Napolitano's fears turned out to be exaggerated, because by the end of the fiscal year, there was an "an estimated $1.5 million surplus."[107] The real problem for Napolitano was that Laffey's last budget, which had been approved by the Democrat-controlled city council, had used about $4 million from various stabilization accounts. Napolitano called Laffey's last budget a "political budget" and decried its reliance on one-time revenues.[108] Using this as his justification, Napolitano proposed raising property taxes by over 5 percent.

Raising taxes is never popular, but raising taxes while not giving any additional funding to the schools proved particularly problematic for Napolitano. In Cranston, there are residents who care more about education than about tax increases, and then there are residents who care more about lower taxes than education funding. In this case, Napolitano had angered both groups. Some residents attacked his tax increase, while others attacked his level funding of the schools, and Republicans attacked him for breaking his campaign pledges. In the end, the Democrat-controlled city council passed a budget that slightly lowered the proposed tax increase and increased school funding by only $1 million. The school committee, led by former mayor Michael Traficante, contended it was inadequate and would later legally challenge it.

Although Napolitano's first budget led to some controversy, Napolitano's overall objective was to avoid controversy—in particular, controversy leading to litigation. Throughout his tenure, Napolitano attempted to settle disputes rather than litigate because he believed "controversy costs money."[109] In the area of labor relations, Napolitano quickly dismissed Laffey's outside labor lawyer, who had won many of Laffey's battles with the city's labor unions, and replaced him with a lawyer who charged less but who had "represented organized labor for decades."[110] When Napolitano reached an agreement with the firefighters' union, Republicans criticized it for various reasons, such as requiring a lower healthcare co-share from firefighters than what police officers were required to pay, restricting management rights, making it easier for firefighters to claim a disability pension and including September 11 as a paid holiday. One newspaper editorial writer called it "a jaw droppingly generous contract for firefighters loaded with stunning giveaways." Napolitano defended the deal, the city council approved it and Napolitano's labor lawyer said the agreement "built some good will."[111]

Napolitano reached other settlements during his tenure, some of which he paid for by taking on debt. He also reached a very controversial settlement on a harassment claim made by a police officer who had been out of work with pay for a number of years. Napolitano's critics noted that an outside independent investigation conducted by the Laffey administration had found no wrongdoing and that, subsequently, the state retirement board had denied her disability pension for anxiety related to the claim. Napolitano defended his settlement by discussing recently disclosed but disputed e-mails, and Police Chief Stephen McGrath called Laffey's independent investigation inadequate.[112]

Possibly the settlement of which Napolitano was the proudest involved the building of a concrete plant in an Eden Park neighborhood.[113] Cranston is a densely populated city in some areas and has a history of neighbors objecting to business developments that occur near their homes. In 2006, a building permit had been granted to a company to build a concrete plant in an area zoned for industrial use. Neighbors were outraged. During the election, Napolitano pledged to stop the concrete plant, but after becoming mayor, he was prevented from taking any action by one judge, while through mediation, another judge determined that the concrete company's legal claims against the city had merit. Determined to fulfill this campaign promise, Napolitano reached an agreement with the concrete company to pay it $1.9 million to transfer its land over to the city. The city council approved the deal, although some members criticized it, believing that the

A concrete plant in an Eden Park neighborhood sparked objections from nearby neighbors. Construction was halted, and the city paid $1.9 million for flood-prone land. *Courtesy of the City of Cranston.*

city had paid too much for land on a flood plain. Eventually, the city paid the concrete company mostly through the use of open space bond money after the federal government refused to spend money to build affordable housing on the site because it was prone to flooding.

During his tenure, Napolitano was subject to criticism at times for a variety of relatively minor issues, such as refurbishing his office as result of a severe allergy attack, replacing his predecessor's plaque at the new police station and putting up his own plaque instead and allowing his director of administration to drive a city vehicle for personal use. However, the Napolitano administration found large savings when the internal auditor determined that the city had not been adequately enforcing the contract provisions which required retired police officers and firefighters, who had access to comparable alternative healthcare coverage, to utilize that health insurance rather than the city's health insurance. The auditor's efforts produced at least $500,000 in savings.

In 2008, Napolitano decided to propose a budget with no increase in taxes but accomplished this by using $2.7 million of the rainy day fund. Republicans sounded the alarm, and the city council decided not to use the rainy day fund but instead made various adjustments, including budgeting for $1.5 million in potential concessions from the city's unions in order to avoid a tax increase.

The school committee was displeased with this budget as well because it only gave the schools $1 million more to offset a cut in state education aid. More importantly, by this point, a majority on the school committee had already decided to bring a Caruolo action to court in order to obtain over $4 million in additional educational funding from the city. At this point, the school committee had failed to bring its budget in line with what the city had allocated for schools and was running a deficit. As a result, Napolitano and the city council decided to give the School Department $4.1 million out of the rainy day fund as a "loan" in order to pay the School Department's additional expenses. In an effort to avoid litigation, Napolitano reached a settlement with the school committee that would have given the schools up to $3.5 million more and created a panel to give recommendations to the School Department on ways to save money. Although Napolitano pressed the city council to approve the deal, the settlement failed to win passage the first time on a three-to-three vote, and when absent council members voted at a subsequent meeting, it failed on a five-to-four vote. Napolitano was "very disappointed" and gave a "sharp rebuke" to the city council majority.[114]

Crisis

A few weeks later, the "much ballyhooed" efforts to consolidate various school and city departments went "bust" over "turf wars."[115] A month after that, a Superior Court judge delivered a "blistering opinion" that denied the school committee's request and indicated that "the School Committee simply continued to spend money until it had grossly overspent its budget, in violation of Rhode Island law."[116] The decision was later upheld by the Rhode Island Supreme Court, thereby setting precedent for Caruolo actions all across the state.[117] Despite his best efforts to settle the case, Napolitano, the reluctant litigator, had achieved a "courtroom triumph" that would probably be the most important and lasting legacy of his brief two-year term.[118]

This courtroom triumph for Napolitano would not be followed up by an election day triumph. In May 2008, Napolitano decided not to run for reelection in order to spend more time with his family. It would have been a challenging race for Napolitano since a poll produced by a potential Democratic primary opponent showed Napolitano trailing Fung by a wide margin.[119] Napolitano went back to the practice of law.

ALLAN W. FUNG

2009–

Waves of immigration have touched the shores of Cranston for generations. With the election of Allan W. Fung as mayor, a new wave had arrived. Fung was the son of immigrants from Hong Kong who started a restaurant business in Cranston. He became a lawyer, served as a prosecutor and eventually was a lobbyist for an insurance company. He was elected to the Cranston City Council in 2002 and was a staunch ally of Mayor Laffey during the city's financial crisis. In 2006, he ran for mayor on a "message of fiscal conservatism" with a "mild-mannered style" but lost by just seventy-two votes to Mayor Napolitano in a year when Democrats swept the nation.[120] Fung stayed involved and became a vocal critic of Mayor Napolitano's fiscal polices. In 2008, he decided to run again for mayor. Napolitano decided not to run for reelection, and this time, Fung won with 63 percent of the vote, despite another nationwide Democratic wave.

Within days of his inauguration, Fung learned that in order to close a state budget deficit, the governor was proposing to cut $4.6 million in state revenue sharing to Cranston in the middle of the fiscal year. Fung was surprised. He said, "I was expecting to hit the ground running. I wasn't expecting to hit the ground, and hit the ground hard."[121] In addition to this jolt, Fung soon learned that the city was already running a deficit because $1.5 million in union concessions budgeted by the prior city council had not been achieved.

In an effort to achieve concessions and close the budget deficit, Fung reached a three-year agreement with the police union, which he indicated would save $1.6 million over three years through vacancies, higher co-shares for health insurance and an eighteen-month salary freeze. The all-Democratic city council wanted a higher level of co-share, criticized the reduction in the police chief's powers over work schedules and questioned the permanency of the staff reductions. Fung responded that the city council, in December 2008, had approved a contract with the laborers' union that contained no concessions when the city council had budgeted $1.5 million in savings from union concessions for the fiscal year. Eventually, the city council rejected the police contract, and some councilmen began complaining of Fung's "closeness to the police union."[122]

Fung did obtain concessions from other unions later that year, with city council approval. He obtained an agreement with the firefighters' union that he indicated would save $3.3 million over three and a half years through vacancies, higher co-shares for health insurance and a reduction in previously approved raises. A year later, the city council would adopt Fung's four-year agreement with the police union, which Fung said had $2.9 million in concessions and was "structurally" similar to the contract that the council had rejected a year earlier.[123] At about the same time, the city council would adopt another firefighters' contract negotiated by Fung, which permanently reduced the staffing of the fire department by five positions. In his first two years as mayor, Fung indicated that he reduced the city's workforce by about 15 percent.[124] However, despite his best efforts, Fung was unable to close the deficit caused by the mid-year state aid cut. Cranston finished the fiscal year ending June 2009 with a budget deficit. The city had a deficit of $1.7 million, while the schools had a deficit of $3.6 million. As a result, the rainy day fund had been reduced by about a third.

In his first budget, Fung raised property taxes, budgeted for the layoffs of forty-one city employees while leaving twenty-five more positions vacant and gave the School Department less than half of what it had requested. He blamed all of this on the state aid cut and poor budgeting in the prior year. Instead, the city council reduced the tax increase slightly, restored funding to all the jobs Fung had determined to lay off and budgeted for $2.2 million in union concessions again. Fung vetoed the budget but was unanimously overridden by the council. Although the all-Democratic city council was opposing Fung "at every turn," a newspaper reported that Fung was enjoying "something of a honeymoon" with voters because he is a "likable guy" who was seen as "trying" under very difficult circumstances.[125]

Fung explored new approaches and suggested some old ideas to the problems of municipal government. Regarding the schools, he began calling for a new charter school in Cranston, which would be free of the restrictions of a typical public school. He recommended more municipal control over school funding. He explored consolidation with the city of Warwick on senior services, libraries, information technology and animal control. It remains to be seen if any of his proposals will materialize, but in one key area—public employee benefits—Fung achieved a structural change. Fung was able to negotiate a contract with the city hall workers' union that made it the first Rhode Island municipal union to require newly hired employees to join a 401(k) plan rather than a traditional defined benefit plan. Fung hoped Cranston's move would "create a shift in the mindset" regarding public employee pensions.[126]

In 2010, to close the state's recurring deficit, Governor Donald Carcieri proposed to eliminate state reimbursement to cities and towns for the phase out of the car tax, which meant a reduction in state revenues to Cranston of approximately $12 million. In two years, Cranston's state aid would be reduced by approximately $15.8 million. As a result, Fung proposed a budget that reimposed the car tax to make up for lost revenues from the state, raised property taxes, gave the schools $2.8 million more, closed the Budlong Pool and outsourced some jobs at the senior center.

As the budget storm was about to begin, Cranston suffered the Great Flood of 2010. Although this flood was an act of God, some believed that "acts of man" played a role in the extent of flood damage because the amount of "development along the Pawtuxet River and its tributaries over the last

Years of development along rivers played a role in the extent of flood damage caused by Great Flood of 2010, as seen here on Fletcher Avenue. *Courtesy of the* Cranston Herald.

half century" created greater and faster runoff and eliminated terrain that would otherwise absorb and hold rain.[127] For some city council members, overdevelopment was not a concern. At the behest of a developer, the city council came close to increasing the housing density in far-western Cranston by eliminating the two-acre minimum lot requirement in that area. The city council did not approve the change when conservation groups expressed opposition to the proposal, and the city planner disclosed the high cost that would be incurred to provide city services to these new homeowners. Also, a developer with a powerful statehouse politician as his lawyer wanted to build a supermarket near the Pawtuxet River. The developer was able to get the city council to change an ordinance to allow supermarkets to be built on land zoned for heavy commercial and industrial use.[128]

As the new fiscal year approached, the city council passed a budget that had the reimposed car tax but reduced Fung's proposed property tax increase by half and restored funding to various city jobs. The city council did this by taking about $1.5 million from the rainy day fund and by reducing the city's contribution to the police and fire pension fund to about 82 percent of what the actuary had recommended. Fung denounced these changes to the budget. He noted that there was less than $11 million left in the rainy day fund. He said the city council's budgeting practices were "the same type of games that got Cranston in trouble in early 2000s." A city councilman "became heated" and raised his voice "as he defended the Council's decision to dip into the surplus funds to both lessen the property tax increase and to save other programs."[129] Fung vetoed the budget but was again unanimously overridden by the all-Democratic city council.

With that, the campaign season began. During this campaign, Fung's popularity proved insurmountable. In November 2010, Fung won reelection with 76 percent of the vote, but more importantly, the Republicans, who campaigned on the slogan "To get balanced budgets you need a balanced City Council," captured three seats on the city council, thereby completely altering the balance of power on the council. Fung's popularity may have also influenced the decision by the voters to approve a city charter amendment to extend the mayor's term from two years back to four years. Furthermore, the voters approved another city charter amendment that required school labor contracts to be approved by the city council.[130] Apparently, after a decade in which the school committee lost two high-profile lawsuits for more funding and accumulated millions of dollars in debt from deficit spending, the voters had decided to shift more control over school spending to the city.

In January 2011, Cranston held its inaugural ceremony. At this event, which usually emphasizes unity and fresh beginnings, a quarrel among the Democrats surrounding the city council presidency led to public bickering. After some in the audience left in disgust, the inaugural ended with a priest declaring, "May peace and harmony always rule."[131] With that, this chronicle must come to an abrupt and untimely end so as to allow current events to take their natural course and to leave to a future time a history of today, with all its quarrels, to be written.

NOTES

Preface

1. *Cranston City Times*, May 21, 1895.
2. Ibid., May 5, 1925.

Beginnings: 1638–1910

Establishing a Town

1. Robert Elliot Freeman, *Cranston, Rhode Island* (Rhode Island Historical Preservation Commission, 1980), 7.
2. Gladys W. Brayton, *Other Ways and Other Days* (East Providence, RI: Globe Printing Company, 1975), 97.
3. Ibid.

The Cost of Freedom

4. J. Earl Clauson, *Cranston: A Historical Sketch* (Providence, RI: T.S. Hammond, 1904), 18.
5. Ibid., 24–25; Irwin H. Polishook, *Rhode Island and the Union, 1774–1795* (Evanston, IL: Northwestern University Press, 1969), 124–27, 133, 170–73, 189–90, 205, 228–30.

Industrialization and Division

6. One prominent historian, who is sympathetic to the growth of the welfare state, once wrote: "For all their privations many 'welfare mothers' had standards

of living that would have made middle-income Americans in 1900 or 1929 wildly jealous." James Patterson, *America's Struggle Against Poverty, 1900–1985* (Cambridge, MA: Harvard University Press, 1986), 208–09.
7. Peter J. Coleman, *The Transformation of Rhode Island: 1790–1860* (Providence, RI: Brown University Press, 1963), 229–233; Joseph A.A. Coccia, "The Cranston Print Works" (Master's thesis, Rhode Island College of Education, 1955): 102, 108; John K. White, "Alfred E. Smith's Rhode Island Revolution: The Election of 1928," *Rhode Island History* 42 (May 1983): 61.
8. Coleman, *Transformation of Rhode Island*, 74–76.
9. Benjamin Knight, *History of the Sprague Families of Rhode Island* (Santa Cruz, CA: H. Coffin, Book and Job Printer, 1881), 15, 28–29.
10. Ibid., 28; Patrick T. Conley, *Democracy in Decline: Rhode Island's Constitutional Development, 1776–1841* (Providence: Rhode Island Historical Society: 1977), 327.
11. Peter Baldwin, "Becoming a City of Homes: The Suburbanization of Cranston, 1850–1910," *Rhode Island History* 51 (February 1993): 7–10.
12. Some historians, whose viewpoints may be colored by ethnic divisions of the past, have suggested that these eastern sections of Cranston were annexed by Providence in order to ensure Republican control of Cranston. However, at the time of this annexation, Cranston's political allegiances were not to the Republicans but to the Spragues. Baldwin, "Becoming a City of Homes," 7. In fact, the shift in Cranston's allegiance to the Republican Party occurred in 1884. In that year, Cranston elected a Republican to the state senate, supported a Republican presidential nominee and coincided with the departure of Amasa Sprague II, the brother of William Sprague IV, from Cranston town government.
13. William G. McLoughlin, *Rhode Island: A Bicentennial History* (New York: W.W. Norton & Company, 1978), 168.

Becoming a City

14. Scott Molloy, *Trolley Wars* (Washington, D.C.: Smithsonian Institution, n.d.), 61–62, 88.
15. William McLaughlin, "Providence: The Confident Years, 1890–1920," *Rhode Island History* 51 (February 1993): 39–40, 54.
16. Clauson, *Cranston*, 44.
17. Baldwin, "Becoming a City of Homes," 3, 12–13, 16.
18. Ibid., 15, 17.
19. Ibid., 15; *Providence Journal*, March 21, 1942. In Lincoln Steffens's famous expose entitled "Rhode Island: A State for Sale," Sullivan was mentioned for his investigation into corrupt practices on Block Island.

Growth: 1910–1934

Edward M. Sullivan

1. *Cranston City Manual*, 1910, 57–60.
2. *Providence Evening Bulletin*, January 20, 1912. The Republican-appointed police chief, Patrick Trainor, was replaced by James Cuff, who was replaced in 1912 by Daniel Kiernan.
3. *Cranston City Manual*, 1910, 15, 29, 67; 1911, 15; 1912, 11; 1913, 15.
4. Ibid., 1911, 12.
5. *Hardy v. Lee*, 36 R.I. 302 (1914).
6. See *Exeter-West Greenwich Regional School District v. Exeter-West Greenwich Teachers Association*, 489 A.2d 1010 (R.I. 1985).
7. *Cranston City Manual*, 1912, 12–13, 18–20; 1913, 28; *Horton v. Sullivan*, 35 RI 242 (1913); *Cranston Herald*, July 12, 1978.
8. *Cranston News*, August 27, 1924.
9. Sullivan not only switched parties but also seemed to switch roles in Cranston's ongoing political drama. During his youth, Sullivan had inflamed public anger over the spending habits of local government. In his last years, Sullivan "assumed the role of apologist" for Cranston's "stalled, sprawled multi-million dollar sewer construction headache" and criticized the reporting of newspapers over the sewer controversy as sensationalist. *Cranston Herald*, March 27, 1941; August 21, 1941.
10. *Cranston Herald*, March 26, 1942.

John W. Horton

11. *Providence Evening Bulletin*, January 17, 1914. Horton's nominee for police chief was James Cuff, the same man Sullivan had originally appointed as police chief but had subsequently dismissed in 1912.
12. Subsequently, Horton succeeded in having Cuff appointed police chief in 1915.
13. *Cranston City Manual*, 1914, 11, 18.
14. Records of Cranston City Council, 1921–22, 63–67.
15. *Providence Evening Bulletin*, October 16, 1913; October 16, 1914.
16. *Cranston City Manual*, 1914, 11, 14–15.
17. Records of Cranston City Council, 1921–22, 214.

Arthur A. Rhodes

18. Lydia L. Rapoza and Bette Miller, *Images of America: Cranston* (Charleston, SC: Arcadia, 1999), 64.
19. Erwin L. Levine, *Theodore Francis Green: The Rhode Island Years, 1906–1936* (Providence, RI: Brown University Press, 1963), 94–95. The Textile Strike of

1922 was triggered when textile owners, struggling to compete with low-cost, non-union textile mills of the South decided to lower wages and adopted longer hours. George H. Kellner and J. Stanley Lemons, *Rhode Island: The Ocean State* (Sun Valley, CA: American Historical Press, 2004), 85.
20. *Cranston News*, January 5, 1923; February 5, 1923.
21. Ibid., July 11, 1923; September 26, 1923; October 24, 1923; November 14, 1923.
22. Ibid., January 23, 1924; October 22, 1924; January 14, 1925.
23. Ibid., December 30, 1925; April 28, 1926; July 30, 1926; October 27, 1926; December 29, 1926.
24. Ibid., January 9, 1924; January 23, 1924.
25. *Providence Journal*, October 4, 1944.
26. *Cranston News*, July 25, 1928; August 15, 1928. Some newspaper accounts speculated that a split within the Cranston Republican Party also influenced Rhodes' decision not to seek reelection. *Providence Journal*, October 4, 1944; *Cranston Herald*, October 5, 1944.

Frank C. Speck

27. *Cranston News*, August 26, 1928.
28. Ibid., January 9, 1929; October 3, 1928.
29. Ibid., January 9, 1929. It is now commonly recognized that the amount of property tax revenues derived from each new residential development is exceeded by the cost of providing additional municipal services to these new residents.
30. *Cranston News*, January 9, 1929; October 10, 1930.
31. *Providence Journal*, January 26, 1930; *Cranston News*, February 12, 1930.
32. *Cranston News*, February 12, 1930.
33. *Providence Journal*, January 28, 1930; January 29, 1930.
34. *Cranston News*, March 28, 1930); Records of Cranston City Council, 1929–1930, 244.
35. *Cranston News*, February 12, 1930.
36. Ibid., October 10, 1930.

Frederick A. Jones

37. Ibid., January 9, 1931; January 1, 1932; September 30, 1932.
38. Ibid., September 14, 1934.
39. Ibid., September 30, 1932; January 6, 1933.
40. Ibid., November 17, 1933; December 29, 1933.
41. Ibid., September 14, 1934.

Transformation: 1935–1960

Ernest L. Sprague

1. *Cranston News*, January 11, 1935; *Providence Journal*, January 18, 1936.
2. *Providence Journal*, January 18, 1936; February 17, 1936; *Cranston Herald*, October 29, 1936.
3. *Cranston Herald*, May 13, 1937.
4. Ibid., October 31, 1938.
5. Ibid., May 14, 1942; July 2, 1942.
6. Ibid., May 12, 1938; October 20, 1938.
7. Ibid., February 2, 1939.
8. Ibid., February 24, 1939; March 2, 1939.
9. Ibid., May 25, 1939, June 8, 1939.
10. Ibid., May 25, 1939; September 1, 1939.
11. Ibid., October 3, 1940. Walter Sepe had decided not to seek reelection as a state representative in 1938 and instead was elected a city councilman because of the recently implemented prohibition on dual office holding, which prohibited state legislators from also holding a state job. *Cranston Herald*, September 9, 1938.
12. *Cranston Herald*, May 25, 1939.
13. Ibid., June 8, 1939.
14. Ibid., September 1, 1939; July 24, 1941. During its existence, the WPA came under extensive criticism and was the subject of numerous jokes. Because much of the labor on the WPA projects were a "make-work variety," WPA labor was not as cost-effective as work performed by private entities. A common joke of the era regarding the WPA was that its initials stood for "We Piddle Around." James T. Patterson, *America's Struggle Against Poverty, 1900–1985* (Cambridge, MA: Harvard University Press, 1986), 46, 64.
15. *Cranston Herald*, November 18, 1941.
16. *Providence Journal*, August 18, 1942; September 11, 1942; *Cranston Herald*, May 28, 1941; July 24, 1941; August 20, 1942.
17. *Cranston Herald*, March 27, 1941; May 1, 1941; May 28, 1941; July 24, 1941; August 21, 1941; August 20, 1942.
18. Ibid., April 23, 1942; August 20, 1942.
19. *Providence Evening Bulletin*, September 12, 1942.
20. *Cranston Herald*, August 19, 1943.
21. *Providence Journal*, September 1, 1942; *Cranston Herald*, August 6, 1942; September 3, 1942.
22. *Cranston Herald*, September 17, 1942.
23. Ibid., September 24, 1942.

William G. Lind

24. Ibid., September 3, 1942; September 17, 1942; October 29, 1942.
25. *Providence Journal*, September 18, 1944; September 21, 1944.
26. *Cranston Herald*, November 21, 1944; *Providence Journal*, December 6, 2001.
27. *Cranston Herald*, September 21, 1944.
28. *Providence Journal*, November 18, 1944.
29. Ibid., December 16, 1944; *Cranston Herald*, November 21, 1944. Prior to the passage of the firefighters' pension ordinance, a city councilman, speaking to his fellow council members regarding the ordinance, stated that he was "certain not more than six of you have read it" and expressed concern that not "a single councilman" had sought "detailed explanations" or asked "questions about the complicated actuary reports" from a member of the ordinance committee. *Cranston Herald*, November 16, 1944; November 21, 1944.
30. *Cranston Herald*, September 9, 1943; February 24, 1944; *Providence Journal*, September 2, 1942.
31. *Cranston Herald*, September 23, 1943. After a recess, the dispute was resolved. The position of police inspector was established, and Lind appointed John F. Ryan. *Cranston Herald*, September 23, 1943.
32. *Cranston Herald*, October 26, 1944.
33. Ibid.; *Providence Journal*, December 16, 1944.

Hoyt W. Lark

34. *Cranston Herald*, June 8, 1939; *Providence Journal*, September 20, 1942.
35. *Cranston Herald*, March 21, 1946.
36. Ibid., February 20, 1946.
37. Ibid., April 4, 1946; April 25, 1946.
38. Records of the Cranston City Council, 1951–52, 168–69.
39. *Cranston Herald*, September 26, 1946; October 24, 1946.
40. Ibid., October 5, 1944; October 19, 1944; December 23, 1946; January 9, 1947.
41. Freeman, *Cranston, Rhode Island*, 69. About six decades later, the elementary school in Garden City is now on the verge of being classified as poor for purposes of qualifying for additional governmental educational assistance. *Cranston Herald*, May 25, 2011.
42. *Cranston Herald*, January 9, 1947.
43. Ibid., January 9, 1947; November 17, 1949.
44. Ibid., October 5, 1944.
45. Ibid., April 16, 1946; May 28, 1947; August 18, 1949. After the Second World War, Rhode Island not only lost its tax advantage over other states but was also losing its manufacturing jobs at an alarming rate. Kellner and

Lemons, *Rhode Island*, 143. This occurred, in part, because southern states took advantage of the passage of Taft-Hartley in 1947 to enact right-to-work legislation, which hampered unionization.
46. *Providence Journal*, October 25, 1949; *Cranston Herald*, June 22, 1950; September 28, 1950; November 2, 1950); Records of Cranston City Council, 1949–50, 232–33.
47. *Providence Journal*, July 25, 1950; Records of Cranston City Council, 1949–50, 541–42.
48. *Providence Journal*, August 30, 1950.
49. Ibid., August 29, 1950. Future mayor George R. Beane indicated to Bourret's counsel that Bourret's ouster had been discussed at a meeting of the Cranston Republican Party.
50. *Providence Journal*, August 30, 1950; August 31, 1950; September 1, 1950; September 7, 1950; Records of Cranston City Council, 1949–50, 578–88. Of the seven police officers who testified, four of them provided testimony in support of the charges brought against the police chief, while the other three police officers offered testimony in the chief's defense. Of the four police officers who testified against Police Chief Bourret, three of them would eventually become police chiefs themselves. They were Louis Fouchecourt, Anthony J. Moretti and George J. Coffey. Of the three police officers who testified in defense of Police Chief Bourret, two of them would later receive promotions to the rank of captain under Mayor Beane's controversial police reorganization plan in 1954. They were John F. Ryan and Rowland G. Cornell.
51. Frank Tanzi, "A History of Cranston, Rhode Island" (Master's thesis, Boston University School of Education, 1953): 205–06.
52. *Cranston Herald*, October 25, 1951.
53. Ibid., May 6, 1971.

George R. Beane

54. Records of the Cranston City Council, 1953–54, 358; *Providence Journal*, September 22, 1963.
55. *Providence Journal*, December 6, 2001.
56. *Cranston Herald*, March 4, 1954; October 28, 1954; Records of the Cranston City Council, 1949–50, 585.
57. *Providence Journal*, June 29, 1954; *Cranston Herald*, July 1, 1954.
58. Records of the Cranston City Council, 1953–54, 782–80, 818; *Providence Journal*, November 23, 1954.
59. *Providence Journal*, November 23, 1954.

John Turnbull

60. Ibid., January 4, 1955.
61. Ibid., July 26, 1955; July 27, 1955.

62. Turnbull and the Republicans bickered over appointments to the police department, the dismissal of a police officer, the conduct of the public works commissioner, zoning, a mayoral pay raise and even tree care. However, in 1955, Turnbull and the city council did agree that pensions for firefighters and police officers would be based on their average pay over their last three years of service rather than the last five years of service.
63. *Providence Journal*, August 2, 1956.
64. Ibid., August 7, 1956; *Cranston Herald*, October 11, 1956.
65. *Cranston Herald*, January 3, 1957.
66. *Providence Journal*, February 4, 1962; April 19, 1963.
67. *Turnbull v. Commissioner of Internal Revenue*, T.C. Mem 1966–77, 1966 WL 665 (Tax Ct.).
68. *Providence Journal*, October 24, 1992; November 1, 1992.

Earl A. Colvin

69. *Providence Daily Journal*, March 6, 1910.
70. *Cranston Herald*, July 24, 1958; November 20, 1958; February 26, 1959; January 28, 1960.
71. Ibid., April 11, 1957; June 19, 1958.
72. Ibid., January 10, 1957. Colvin also launched a probe into alleged payoffs to city officials for awarding school construction contracts, but a grand jury concluded there was no evidence of criminal conduct.
73. In nearly every single election during the 1950s, the office of mayor was won by a candidate who garnered just 51 percent, while the Republicans won twelve seats and the Democrats won eight seats on the city council. The only exception was the election conducted in 1952.
74. *Cranston Herald*, November 12, 1959.
75. Ibid., December 10, 1959.
76. Ibid., August 28, 1958; February 26, 1959.
77. Ibid., December 10, 1959. Colvin also noted a study that showed Cranston's city employees had higher salaries than employees in other communities and excellent benefits.
78. *Cranston Herald*, May 19, 1960; February 24, 1962; *Providence Journal*, January 18, 1964.
79. *Cranston Herald*, May 26, 1960; February 24, 1962; *Berberian v. Board of Canvassers*, 91 R.I. 49 (1960).
80. *Cranston Herald*, October 30, 1958; October 6, 1960.
81. Ibid., May 19, 1960; September 15, 1960.
82. *Providence Journal*, June 12, 1956; *Cranston Herald*, March 31, 1960; August 11, 1960. Eventually, Leesona would move farther south, all the way to North Carolina.
83. *Cranston Herald*, October 11, 1956.
84. Ibid., August 25, 1960.

85. Ibid., September 1, 1960; September 15, 1960.
86. Ibid., September 1, 1960; September 29, 1960; October 20, 1960.
87. *Providence Journal*, February 18, 1964. Colvin was born in 1892, the year that the streetcar system was electrified, which helped change Cranston into a suburban city.
88. *Cranston Herald*, March 31, 1960.

CHALLENGES: 1961–1984

Francis R. Dailey

1. *Providence Journal*, December 16, 1997.
2. From 1884 until 1960, Cranston consistently voted for Republicans at the presidential level, with the exception of 1912.
3. *Providence Journal*, October 1, 1961.
4. Records of the Cranston City Council, 1961–62, 100, 136–38.
5. *Providence Journal*, September 25, 1962. This was the first law enacted in Rhode Island that required collective bargaining with public employee unions.
6. *Cranston Herald*, October 26, 1950; October 20, 1960; May 31, 1962.
7. *Providence Journal*, September 25, 1962.
8. Ibid.
9. Ibid., October 23, 1962.
10. Records of the Cranston City Council, 1961–62, 616–17.
11. *Providence Journal*, September 25, 1962.
12. *Cranston Herald*, October 4, 1962; November 1, 1962.
13. Records of the Cranston City Council, 1961–62, 708–09.
14. Mayor James DiPrete Jr. nominated, and the city council confirmed, Gibbs as police chief.
15. Pension Records of Francis R. Dailey from ERSRI. Dailey just barely qualified for this pension. He received this pension because he was mayor when the pension plan went into effect on January 1, 1963. *Providence Journal*, April 27, 1963.
16. While enjoying retirement, Dailey began to express concern over government spending by calling Franklin Roosevelt the "first Santa Claus" and warning of "a day of reckoning" because "there's no free ride." *Cranston Herald*, January 7, 1976.

James DiPrete Jr.

17. *Cranston Herald*, February 21, 1962.
18. *Providence Journal*, November 7, 1962.
19. *Cranston Herald*, February 21, 1962.
20. *Providence Journal*, November 19, 1993.

21. *Cranston Herald*, March 30, 1961.
22. Cranston's population grew from 66,766 in 1960 to 74,287 by 1970.
23. Records of the Cranston City Council, 1963–64, 18, 140; *Cranston Herald*, April 25, 1963; January 9, 1964; *Providence Journal*, July 14, 1963; January 3, 1965.
24. Records of the Cranston City Council, 1969–70, 13; *Cranston Herald*, December 13, 1962; February 20, 1964; May 21, 1970.
25. *Providence Journal*, April 1, 1963.
26. Cranston's police officers were divided on organizing a union. *Providence Journal*, August 22, 1963.
27. *Fox v. Personnel Appeal Board*, 99 R.I. 566 (1965); *Henry v. Thomas*, 100 R.I. 564 (1966).
28. *Providence Journal*, September 19, 1963; September 20, 1963; September 21, 1963.
29. *Morgan v. Thomas*, 98 R.I. 204 (1964).
30. *Providence Journal*, April 19, 1964; January 3, 1965; *Cranston Herald*; January 20, 1966. In 1966, Police Chief Louis Fouchecourt would retire from the police force to become the executive director of the Cranston Housing Authority after the departure of former Mayor Francis Dailey. *Providence Journal*, May 17, 1966.
31. *Cranston Herald*, October 1, 1964; November 10, 1965; April 27, 1967; *Providence Journal*, January 3, 1965; May 14, 1968.
32. *Providence Journal*, September 28, 1964. Within a few years, one newspaper editorial would criticize the importance placed on the seniority system at the police department, where duties were "meted out by seniority and not by capabilities," by indicating that it brought about a "sick attitude" in which "enthusiasm is resented" and "energies fade." *Cranston Herald*, April 27, 1967.
33. *Cranston Herald*, June 6, 1966; September 10, 1968; *Providence Journal*, January 2, 1966; January 9, 1966.
34. *Providence Journal*, November 19, 1993. The passage of the primary election law in 1947 also fundamentally shifted power away from the party bosses. The power of Cranston's last party bosses, Daniels and Sepe, ended as a result of an unfavorable primary election.
35. *Cranston Herald*, August 24, 1967; August 31, 1967; November 22, 1967; May 7, 1968; May 14, 1968.
36. Ibid., January 12, 1967.
37. Ibid., July 20, 1967.
38. *Providence Journal*, July 16, 1967; August 4, 1967; August 11, 1967; *Cranston Herald*, August 10, 1967; November 22, 1967.
39. *Cranston Herald*, July 20, 1967.
40. *Providence Journal*, August 7, 1967; *Cranston Herald*, August 10, 1967; August 24, 1967.
41. *Providence Journal*, August 25, 1967; August 30, 1967; *Cranston Herald*, November 2, 1967.
42. *Providence Journal*, May 22, 1968.
43. *Cranston Herald*, November 22, 1967.

44. Ibid., January 18, 1968; February 29, 1968.
45. *Providence Journal*, November 4, 1967.
46. Ibid., May 3, 1968; May 29, 1968.
47. Ibid., June 5, 1968.
48. Ibid., May 7, 1968; May 11, 1968.
49. Records of the City Council, 1967–68, 762, 791; Records of the City Council, 1969–70, 283.
50. *Providence Journal*, October 30, 1968.
51. Ibid., October 31, 1968.
52. Ibid., November 3, 1968.
53. *Providence Journal*, November 6, 1968.
54. Records of the City Council, 1965–66, 271–79. These ordinances were adopted at the same time the city council and DiPrete approved contracts that made Cranston police and firefighters the second-highest-paid safety service employees in Rhode Island. *Providence Journal*, June 29, 1965.
55. *Providence Journal*, March 8, 1992.
56. Records of the City Council, 1965–66, 271–79. In 1964, DiPrete and the city council approved of an ordinance that increased the average pension payment from 50 percent to 55 percent of a police officer's or firefighter's salary at retirement. The ordinance adopted in 1965 caused the increase to 55 percent to be delayed until the retiree reached age fifty-five.
57. *Cranston Herald*, April 17, 1969.
58. Records of the City Council, 1969–70, 281–84.
59. *Trice v. Cranston*, 110 R.I. 724 (1972).
60. *Providence Journal*, March 8, 1992; December 6, 2001.
61. Records of the Cranston City Council, 1963, 137.
62. *Cranston Herald*, May 21, 1980. In 1964, Reagan's famed speech endorsing Goldwater launched Reagan's political career. In that same year, DiPrete had garnered national media attention when he repudiated Barry Goldwater, the Republican presidential nominee, and labeled him a "fascist." *Providence Journal*, December 17, 1969. In politics, consistency is a quality to which only some aspire and which even fewer ever acquire.
63. *Providence Journal*, January 22, 1986.
64. Ibid., January 19, 1986.
65. Ibid., November 19, 1993.

James L. Taft Jr.

66. *Cranston Herald*, January 7, 1971.
67. Records of the City Council, 1971–72, 7–10, 99 (I-7 of the budget).
68. *Cranston Herald*, April 22, 1971; *Providence Journal*, August 11, 1971; February 26, 1998. Litigation commenced, and a few years later, the city received $100,000 from a legal settlement arising over the faulty construction.
69. *Cranston Herald*, September 21, 1977; January 11, 1978.

70. Ibid., May 24, 1973; April 4, 1974; April 25, 1974; October 31, 1974.
71. *Providence Journal Almanac*, 1971, 95; 1979, 72. Cranston's population decreased from 74,287 in 1970 to 71,992 by 1980.
72. *Cranston Herald*, May 17, 1973; November 27, 1974; June 19, 1975. Transvan, a transportation program for the elderly, was originally only a demonstration project funded by the federal government. But when federal funding for Transvan ended, the program continued on, thereby demonstrating how difficult it is to end a government program once it starts.
73. *Cranston Herald*, September 21, 1977; January 4, 1978; January 11, 1978; September 26, 1979.
74. Records of the Cranston City Council, 1973–74, 523 (I-5); *Cranston Herald*, April 4, 1974; April 25, 1974; August 17, 1977; *Cranston Today*, April 10, 1974.
75. Records of the Cranston City Council, 1975–76, 12; *Cranston Herald*, January 9, 1975.
76. *Cranston Herald*, June 26, 1975; *Cranston Herald-Today*, September 3, 1975; September 24, 1975. On another occasion, in 1978, a Cranston teachers' strike delayed the opening of schools for a few days until teachers got a 6.5 percent salary increase. *Cranston Herald*, December 27, 1978.
77. *Cranston Herald-Today*, November 26, 1975; December 17, 1975.
78. Ibid., December 31, 1975.
79. Ibid., April 7, 1976.
80. Ibid., January 5, 1977; March 9, 1977. According to Taft, Coffey had tape-recorded a conversation between Taft and Coffey. Also, Taft was highly critical of Coffey's oversight of the Cranston dog pound.
81. *Cranston Herald*, February 21, 1979.
82. Ibid., March 9, 1977.
83. *Cranston Herald-Today*, March 9, 1977; March 30, 1977; April 6, 1977. One minor issue that garnered major attention was how Taft filled up his car with gasoline from the police garage pump.
84. *Cranston Herald*, January 4, 1978; February 1, 1978.
85. Ibid., October 25, 1978; Records of the City Council, 1977–78, 585.
86. Four of the Democrats on the city council in 1973 who were pushing to study the pension system had voted in 1969 for the ordinance that lowered the service requirement to receive a pension from twenty-five years to twenty years for police and firefighters.
87. *Cranston Herald*, November 16, 1977; February 1, 1978; October 25, 1978; *Providence Journal*, December 6, 2001.
88. *Providence Journal*, May 6, 1989; June 18, 1992.
89. Ibid., July 31, 1988; August 2, 1988; August 26, 1988.
90. Ibid., February 4, 1989; September 17, 1994.
91. Records of the City Council, 1977–78, 186.

Edward D. DiPrete

92. Records of Cranston City Council, 1979–80, 11; *Cranston Herald*, January 3, 1979.
93. In one year, although Cranston's tax rate was reduced due to a revaluation, property tax bills generally increased. *Cranston Herald*, May 17, 1984.
94. *Cranston Herald*, April 18, 1979.
95. *Picerne v. DiPrete*, 428 A.2d 1074 (R.I. 1981).
96. *Cranston Herald*, May 2, 1979; *Providence Journal*, December 27, 1983; July 20, 1986.
97. *Cranston Herald*, March 18, 1982; April 1, 1982; January 19, 1984; *Providence Journal*, January 17, 1984.
98. *Cranston Herald*, August 8, 1979; *Providence Journal Almanac*, 1921, 127.
99. *Cranston Herald*, April 2, 1980; October 8, 1981; July 15, 1982.
100. Ibid., April 4, 1979.
101. Ibid., April 11, 1979; April 18, 1979.
102. Ibid., January 24, 1979; May 21, 1981; *Providence Journal*, December 27, 1984.
103. Records of the Cranston City Council, 1981–82, 187; *Cranston Herald*, May 21, 1981; July 15, 1982.
104. Records of the Cranston City Council, 1971–72, 499, 598, Res.72-66, Res.72-108.
105. *Cranston Herald-Today*, December 10, 1975; *Providence Journal*, March 4, 1992.
106. *City of Cranston v. Hall*, 118 R.I. 20 (1976).
107. *Cranston Herald*, October 9, 1980. The arbitrator was Rita Michaelson, the wife of Julius Michaelson, who was the sponsor of legislation to extend collective bargaining rights to Rhode Island teachers in 1966. From 1968 until 1994, the neutral arbitrator on the three-person arbitration panel was selected by the chief justice of the Rhode Island Supreme Court. A mayor of a neighboring city noted that during this era, "the court would always appoint a third arbitrator who was a union-oriented individual." *Providence Journal*, June 5, 2011. At this time, the chief justice of the Rhode Island Supreme Court was selected by the Rhode Island General Assembly, which was dominated by Democrats. From 1966 to 1976, Thomas Roberts, the brother of Democratic governor Dennis Roberts, was chief justice. In one case, Roberts, alone in dissent, asserted that "public employees have a constitutionally protected right to strike." *School Committee of Westerly v. Westerly Teachers Association*, 111 R.I. 96, 111 (1973). From 1976 to 1986, Joseph Bevilacqua, former Democratic Speaker of the Rhode Island House of Representatives, was chief justice. From 1986 to 1993, Thomas Fay, former Democratic chairman of the Rhode Island House Judiciary Committee, was chief justice.
108. *Cranston Herald*, October 9, 1980; October 16, 1980.
109. Ibid., June 25, 1981; *Providence Journal*, April 4, 1986; December 12, 1998.

110. *Cranston Herald*, April 14, 1983. Two other Cranston mayors, Stephen Laffey and Allan Fung, also advocated for the removal of retirement benefits from the scope of collective bargaining for public employees. *Providence Journal*, February 18, 2005; March 28, 2011.
111. *Cranston Herald*, April 30, 1981; June 2, 1983.
112. *Providence Journal*, March 8, 1992.
113. *Cranston Herald*, December 1, 1983.
114. Ibid., February 23, 1984.
115. *Providence Journal*, June 11, 1986.
116. Ibid., December 31, 1990; August 9, 1998.
117. Ibid., August 9, 1998; December 5, 1999; December 13, 1998; April 10, 2004; November 9, 2008.
118. *Providence Journal*, November 4, 1984; December 31, 1990; December 5, 1999.

CRISIS: 1985–PRESENT

Michael A. Traficante

1. *Providence Journal*, March 13, 1985.
2. From 1980 to 1990, Cranston's population grew from 71,060 to 79,269, with most of this growth occurring in western Cranston.
3. *Providence Journal*, March 12, 1985.
4. Records of the Cranston City Council, 1984, 127; 1985, 167; *Providence Journal*, April 2, 1985; May 10, 1985.
5. *Providence Journal*, October 15, 1986.
6. Ibid., April 3, 1987.
7. Ibid., January 11, 1998. Regardless of party affiliation, if a political organization is dependent on government patronage to survive, it will seek to at least maintain, if not expand, government. For as the powers of government increase, so does the power of those who control it.
8. Records of the Cranston City Council, 1989, 233 (I-6).
9. *Providence Journal*, October 21, 1988.
10. Ibid., March 31, 1989; April 3, 1989; May 16, 1989; May 18, 1989.
11. Ibid., December 13, 1989; December 19, 1989; January 24, 1989.
12. Ibid., May 16, 1991.
13. Ibid., April 8, 1992; April 23, 1992; May 9, 1992; June 9, 1992; June 12, 1992.
14. Ibid., July 29, 1992; September 29, 1992.
15. Ibid., October 23, 1992.
16. Ibid., June 13, 1992.
17. Ibid., October 14, 1992; December 7, 1992.
18. Ibid., November 4, 1992.

19. Ibid., April 2, 1993.
20. Ibid., January 4, 1993; May 5, 1993; June 3, 1993; July 6, 1994.
21. Ibid., (December 1/1993, 6/21/1994).
22. Ibid., March 21, 1993; March 23, 1993.
23. Ibid., February 16, 1994; March 28, 1994; March 29, 1994.
24. Ibid., January 26, 1994; June 16, 1994.
25. Ibid., March 6, 1985; March 5, 1999; October 31, 2000.
26. Ibid., October 14, 1994; October 31, 1994. Cranston's fire chief Albert Tedeschi "derided" these volunteer firefighters by calling them "boy scouts." *Providence Journal*, May 12, 1994.
27. *Cranston Herald*, March 12, 1980; September 17, 1980.
28. *Providence Journal*, June 20, 1994.
29. Ibid., April 4, 1995; April 18, 1995; April 24, 1995.
30. Ibid., April 2, 1996.
31. Ibid., April 10, 1996; April 12, 1996; April 19, 1996; April 23, 1996; April 24, 1996.
32. Ibid., April 29, 1996; May 7, 1996; May 8, 1996; May 10, 1996; May 16, 1996.
33. Ibid., August 27, 1996; August 28, 1996.
34. Ibid., November 6, 1996; November 7, 1996.
35. Police officers and firefighters who retired under the new state pension plan would not get a 5 percent increase in their pension when they turned fifty-five years of age. Also, their pension would be based on their final year of compensation rather than their pay at the very last moment before retirement.
36. *Providence Journal*, November 29, 1996.
37. Ibid., August 1, 1996.
38. Police officers and firefighters who retired under the new state pension plan also received a 3 percent cost of living increase every year in their pensions.
39. Ibid., March 28, 2003. In addition, the pension contributions for firefighters under the city pension plan increased from 3 to 9 percent of their salaries.
40. *Providence Journal*, August 18, 1995; July 9, 1998.
41. Ibid., April 3, 1997; April 9, 1997.
42. Ibid., October 21, 1997.
43. Ibid., October 24, 1997.
44. Ibid., November 30, 1997; December 2, 1997.
45. Ibid., October 21, 1998; November 5, 1998; November 29, 1999.
46. Ibid., March 5, 1999.

John O'Leary

47. *Providence Journal*, November 4, 1998; November 6, 1998; November 18, 1998.
48. Ibid., March 31, 1999; April 1, 1999; May 3, 1999; April 12, 2002.
49. Ibid., March 31, 2000; May 4, 2000; May 5, 2000; May 9, 2000; May 10, 2000; May 11, 2000; May 12, 2000.

50. Ibid., May 7, 1999.
51. Ibid., December 8, 1999; December 16, 1999; January 12, 2000.
52. Ibid., February 4, 2000.
53. Ibid., June 30, 2000.
54. Ibid., August 31, 2000.
55. Ibid., October 2, 2000.
56. Ibid., November 8, 2000; November 9, 2000.
57. Ibid., June 27, 2001.
58. Ibid., October 17, 2001.
59. Ibid., October 23, 2001; October 31, 2001.
60. Ibid., April 14, 2002; March 19, 2002; October 31, 2001; October 30, 2001; October 18, 2001.
61. Ibid., March 21, 2002; April 4, 2002; April 9, 2002; April 10, 2002.
62. Ibid., May 15, 2002.
63. Ibid., June 6, 2002; June 12, 2002.
64. Ibid., August 20, 2002; September 5, 2002.
65. Ibid., September 12, 2002.
66. Ibid., November 9, 2002; November 13, 2002.
67. Ibid., January 18, 1999; September 24, 2002; January 3, 2003; January 2, 2003.
68. Ibid., October 29, 2006.
69. Ibid., January 30, 2003.
70. Ibid., December 6, 2002.
71. Ibid., January 5, 1999; January 3, 2003.

Stephen P. Laffey

72. *Providence Journal*, December 8, 2002; February 22, 2004; December 19, 2006.
73. Ibid., October 22, 2002; *Memphis Business Journal*, May 4, 2001.
74. *Providence Journal*, December 9, 2002.
75. Ibid., December 24, 2002; January 2, 2003.
76. Ibid., January 7, 2003.
77. *Cranston Herald*, June 26, 1975; *Providence Journal*, April 1, 1987.
78. *Providence Journal*, March 27, 2003; May 11, 2003.
79. Ibid., October 8, 2002.
80. Ibid., August 19, 2003.
81. Ibid., September 23, 2003.
82. Ibid., September 27, 2003.
83. Ibid., March 9, 2004.
84. Ibid., March 10, 2004.
85. Ibid., August 1, 2003; September 6, 2003; September 23, 2003; September 5, 2003.
86. Ibid., January 26, 2004; January 7, 2004.
87. Ibid., February 19, 2004; March 19, 2004; May 11, 2004. An experienced labor attorney for the city of Cranston indicated that arbitrators have an

incentive to support unions in arbitration because union leaders are in power longer and therefore might rehire them, while government officials may change with elections. *GoLocalProv*, June 30, 2011.
88. *Providence Journal*, June 17, 2004; June 26, 2004; June 29, 2004; July 1, 2004; September 9, 2004.
89. Ibid., August 25/2004, 8/31/2004, 9/1/2004).
90. Ibid., September 15, 2004.
91. Ibid., September 16, 2004.
92. Ibid., January 4, 2005.
93. Ibid., January 12, 2005.
94. Also, the popularity of public employee unions declined in Rhode Island during this time period. For instance, one poll conducted in 2010 indicated that 57 percent of voters thought labor unions had too much influence over state government. (WPRI 12 poll conducted in January 2010).
95. Reductions in 2009 and 2010 to the pension benefits of state employees and teachers affected even vested employees.
96. The results of the 2010 election in Rhode Island seemed to indicate that public employee unions may have regained some lost influence. Lincoln Chafee, an Independent, won the governorship with 36 percent of the vote because of his support from teachers' unions. Also, the East Providence School Committee, which had unilaterally reduced the pay and benefits of teachers, was swept out of office through the efforts of public employee unions. Lastly, some state legislators who had voted to reduce the pension benefits of vested public employees were defeated in Democratic Party primaries due to the efforts of public employees unions.
97. The judge ruled that because the pension benefits of retired police officers and firefighters are permissible subjects of collective bargaining, once granted, they can be changed only through collective bargaining. *City of Cranston v. IBPO 301*, No. 04-1043; *City of Cranston v. IAFF*, No. 04-1646, slip op. at 16-19 (Rhode Island Supreme Court, February 11, 2005).
98. Laffey's tendency to use belittling rhetoric caused some sharp words to be fired back at him. For instance, city council president Peter Pastore suggested that if the city was spending money on soundproofing the mayor's office, it should also spend money on "padded walls." *Providence Journal*, January 7, 2004.
99. *Providence Journal*, December 1, 2005.
100. Ibid., October 19, 2006.
101. Ibid., September 13, 2006.
102. During the campaign in 2006, Lincoln Chafee had advertisements criticizing Laffey for raising property taxes, but once Chafee became governor in 2011 and proposed an expansion of the sales tax, he credited Laffey for raising property tax increases.
103. *Providence Journal*, September 30, 2003; September 9, 2004.
104. Ibid., February 22, 2004; September 28, 2004; January 6, 2005; April 26, 2005.

Michael T. Napolitano

105. *Providence Journal*, April 19, 2006.
106. Ibid., January 30, 2007.
107. *Cranston Herald*, August 29, 2007.
108. *Providence Journal*, February 27, 2007.
109. Ibid., January 25, 2007; October 10, 2008.
110. Ibid., October 10, 2008.
111. Ibid., June 28, 2007; July 5, 2007; August 7, 2007; August 20, 2007; August 22, 2007; August 28, 2007; September 6, 2007; October 10, 2008. Later that year, a study showed that Rhode Island spent the most per capita than any other state on fire protection, and Cranston firefighters received the highest average pay in Rhode Island.
112. *Providence Journal*, March 28, 2008; April 4, 2008; June 12, 2008; October 10, 2008.
113. Ibid., May 28, 2008.
114. Ibid., July 2, 2008; July 9, 2008; July 11, 2008; October 10, 2008.
115. Ibid., July 25, 2008.
116. Ibid., September 4, 2008.
117. *School Committee of City of Cranston v. Bergin-Andrews*, 984 A.2d 629 (Rhode Island, 2009).
118. *Providence Journal*, October 10, 2008.
119. Ibid., June 13, 2008.

Allan W. Fung

120. *Providence Journal*, November 10, 2008.
121. Ibid., January 11, 2009.
122. Ibid., April 22, 2009; June 24, 2009; August 26, 2009. At about this time, Police Chief Stephen McGrath resigned a few days after a no-confidence vote by the police union. This was not the first time a Cranston police chief had received a vote of no confidence from the police union. Police Chief Augustine Comella Jr. resigned from his post about a year after he received the no-confidence vote from the police union.
123. *Providence Journal*, April 17, 2010; May 13, 2010.
124. Ibid., June 10, 2010.
125. Ibid., July 19, 2009.
126. Ibid., April 11, 2010.
127. Ibid.
128. Ibid., June 20, 2010.
129. *Cranston Herald*, June 17, 2010.
130. *Providence Journal*, November 3, 2010.
131. *Cranston Herald*, January 6, 2011.

Index

B

Beane, George 58, 59, 60, 83, 145
budget 25, 33, 34, 40, 45, 50, 56, 59, 60, 65, 67, 70, 71, 72, 75, 76, 84, 85, 86, 87, 88, 89, 90, 93, 98, 99, 101, 102, 105, 107, 108, 111, 113, 114, 116, 117, 118, 120, 122, 126, 129, 130, 132, 134, 135, 136, 149

C

charter 20, 21, 28, 52, 61, 66, 67, 68, 72, 73, 74, 76, 83, 88, 98, 105, 112, 127, 135, 137
Colvin, Earl 62, 63, 64, 65, 66, 67, 68, 72, 73, 74, 75, 146, 147

D

Dailey, Francis 67, 68, 69, 70, 71, 72, 147, 148
development 19, 37, 55, 56, 75, 76, 86, 91, 131, 135
DiPrete, Edward 87, 89, 90, 91, 92, 93, 94, 95, 96, 97, 98, 99, 101, 102, 105

DiPrete, James, Jr. 73, 74, 75, 76, 77, 78, 79, 80, 81, 82, 83, 90

F

firefighters 51, 54, 59, 60, 71, 72, 78, 80, 81, 84, 93, 94, 95, 101, 102, 105, 108, 110, 114, 115, 118, 122, 124, 125, 126, 127, 130, 132, 134, 144, 146, 149, 150, 153, 155, 156
Fung, Allan 126, 129, 133, 134, 135, 136, 137, 152

G

General Assembly 10, 11, 13, 14, 15, 20, 21, 32, 40, 43, 45, 47, 51, 66, 71, 76, 80, 86, 94, 102, 110, 116, 151

H

Horton, John 26, 27, 28, 29, 30, 31, 32, 141

J

Jones, Frederick 38, 39, 40, 41

INDEX

L

Laffey, Stephen 112, 118, 119, 120, 121, 122, 123, 124, 125, 126, 127, 128, 129, 130, 131, 133, 152, 155
Lark, Hoyt 51, 52, 53, 54, 55, 56, 57, 58, 59
Lind, William 50, 51, 52, 53, 144

N

Napolitano, Michael 112, 129, 130, 131, 132, 133, 134

O

O'Leary, John 112, 113, 114, 115, 116, 117, 118, 119, 120, 121, 129

P

pension(s) 44, 45, 46, 50, 51, 52, 54, 57, 59, 66, 71, 72, 81, 82, 83, 88, 94, 95, 96, 107, 110, 111, 116, 117, 118, 121, 122, 125, 126, 127, 130, 131, 135, 136, 144, 146, 147, 149, 150, 153, 155
police 17, 23, 24, 26, 27, 28, 34, 37, 44, 50, 51, 52, 54, 55, 56, 57, 59, 60, 71, 72, 74, 76, 77, 78, 79, 80, 81, 82, 84, 86, 88, 93, 95, 101, 108, 109, 110, 114, 115, 116, 117, 122, 125, 126, 127, 130, 132, 134, 136, 141, 144, 145, 146, 148, 149, 150, 155, 156

R

Rhodes, Arthur 31, 32, 33, 34, 35, 36, 37, 38, 142

S

school committee 25, 39, 40, 44, 65, 67, 74, 75, 76, 86, 90, 93, 98, 112, 113, 114, 122, 123, 124, 126, 130, 132, 133, 137, 151, 155, 156
services 17, 18, 20, 24, 25, 28, 29, 30, 31, 32, 34, 37, 39, 56, 58, 64, 74, 76, 84, 85, 88, 89, 91, 95, 98, 99, 100, 105, 108, 111, 112, 114, 116, 124, 135, 136, 142
sewer 30, 32, 33, 36, 46, 47, 48, 49, 50, 51, 53, 55, 59, 62, 74, 78, 91, 92, 96, 100, 104, 111, 141
Speck, Frank 36, 37, 38, 39
Sprague, Ernest 43, 44, 45, 46, 47, 48, 49, 50, 51, 53, 54
Sullivan, Edward 20, 21, 23, 24, 25, 26, 28, 32, 36, 37, 39, 40, 49, 61, 140, 141

T

Taft, James, Jr. 83, 84, 85, 86, 87, 88, 89, 90, 93, 97, 145, 150
Traficante, Michael 97, 98, 99, 100, 101, 102, 103, 104, 105, 106, 107, 108, 109, 110, 111, 112, 117, 119, 128, 130
Turnbull, John 60, 61, 62, 63, 64, 146

U

union(s) 65, 68, 69, 71, 76, 77, 78, 79, 80, 82, 86, 88, 93, 95, 101, 103, 104, 105, 109, 114, 115, 117, 118, 122, 124, 125, 126, 127, 128, 130, 134, 135, 142, 148, 151, 155, 156

About the Author

Steven Frias, a Brown University graduate and a history enthusiast, is an attorney specializing in public utility, telecommunications and administrative law. He is active in both local and state politics, has advised two Cranston mayors and has served on various local boards. He currently serves on the board of directors of the Cranston Historical Society. His op-eds on historical events or current events from a historical perspective have been published in both the *Providence Journal* and the *Cranston Herald*.

Visit us at
www.historypress.net